Joan
4/1/53

GOD KEEPS AN OPEN HOUSE

GOD KEEPS AN OPEN HOUSE

By *Lilian Lauferty*

THE BOBBS-MERRILL COMPANY, INC.

Publishers

INDIANAPOLIS NEW YORK

PRINTED IN THE UNITED STATES OF AMERICA

Library of Congress Catalog Card Number: 52-6642

First Edition

O foolish ones, put by your care!
Where wants are many, joys are few;
And at the wilding springs of peace,
God keeps an open house for you.

—Bliss Carman, "The Mendicants"

CONTENTS

CONTENTS—Continued

PAGE

PART 3

REAL-*ization: Learn to Cultivate Your Eternal Values*

FOREWORD

THE BURNING BUSH

. . . and be ready always to give an answer to every man that asketh you a reason of the hope that is in you . . .

—I PETER 3:15

I FOUND GOD IN CENTRAL PARK. I was not looking for God. I doubted the existence of a Supreme Being. From my point of view there was no indication of any power or purpose in the universe beyond that of an impersonal force dedicated to such matters as keeping the earth in its orbit, the seasons in a regimented march, and the sun and moon and stars from crashing into one another.

"None but myself shall I meet on the highway of Fate!" was my creed and it did not satisfy me. I was vastly tired of myself and of the sardonic fate which had just snatched from my grasp everything that counted. Life had always played cat-and-mouse with me. Now the cat had pounced.

Looking back into the shadows, I could not find any encouragement to look forward or to go forward. So I sat down on a park bench and gave myself over to the remembrance of things I needed to forget.

When I was five Grandma persuaded my parents to give up the gay little house where I had a playroom and move to the big formal house where she had a conservatory. Grandpa said he was old and tired and needed his only son to look after him and the bank. So Father gave up his own store and tried to be a banker instead of a merchant and never had time to play Rock of Ages, with the sewing machine draped to look like a rock. When Father had an afternoon free, Grandpa always wanted him to drive out to the ball park or the race track, but he did not want a little girl tagging along.

It was not easy to be happy in a house where Grandma had a conservatory but where I had no playroom; it was harder when Grandma and Grandpa died and the house was sold to meet the proud bequests Grandpa had made to his three daughters, who did not need the money except to impress their rich husbands. Father too was proud, so he did not protest the will, which left him nothing but the heavy Victorian furniture he could not afford to move. Then, because he thought it would be humiliating to be a poor man in the town where he had been a leading merchant and the president of the Businessmen's Exchange and where everyone knew us, we moved to an Eastern city where we did not know anyone.

It hurt to be uprooted from the big yard where roses arched above the front gate, lilacs leaned over the porch and russet apple trees shaded the summer kitchen. It hurt when the advertising-novelty business Father had established in the New England territory, where his firm had never been able to gain a foothold, was taken from him and turned over to a junior executive. The fact that "Junior" was the son of the chief stockholder, had been a playboy till Father made him a businessman, and had once wanted to be Father's son-in-law added to the irony of the defeat. But what hurt most was the quickening awareness that the daddy I had adored was a dreamer and that the mother I had taken for granted always paid gallantly for his dreams.

At sixteen I went to college knowing my success was Mother's dream and that the way to make it come true was to be a successful writer. She based her expectation on the fact that before I was nine the home-town press had published a book of my verse and had called it *Poems of Childhood.* I thought her dream had come true when Prexy read two of my poems aloud in assembly and called the unidentified writer a young Christina Rossetti. After that the college monthly published my verse; but I could not sell it to any of the national magazines, and I was not asked to join either of the literary societies. All this added to my confusion and sense that life was made up of bitter ironies.

So my poetry took on a tinge of Poe's melancholy, and it got me a job when it was imperative that I have one. Father had just gone through a business crisis which destroyed his confidence and his spirit; I had gone through a bitter romance which threatened to be equally destructive, and we had moved to a dreary two-family house on a court. But Mother's spirit was unbroken, her courage was our prop, and her resourcefulness led to my meeting the famous newspaper editor Arthur Brisbane and to his publishing my poems on the editorial page of the New York *Evening Journal*. The newspaper paid ten dollars apiece for them, so I turned them out assiduously and with such a sense of routine that they degenerated from verse to rhyme to doggerel.

But before this was apparent the fabulous A.B. broke down Father's reluctance to let his only daughter leave home and become a wage earner. "The girl has a marketable talent; let her take it to the market place," Brisbane said. So I set off to begin my career in New York as the Girl Reporter of the *Journal* at a staff writer's pay of thirty dollars a week, and I sent ten of it home. Life in a hall bedroom was a great adventure. I had beaux galore and soon became engaged to a fascinating philanderer who boasted that he hadn't known he was a marrying man till I came along.

About this time Father had a complete breakdown, and his already depleted savings were drained to pay doctor and nurses. So I began writing half a dozen newspaper features under almost as many by-lines. My fiancé insisted that I ought to make my own name instead of scribbling under a lot of names copyrighted by the newspaper syndicate. But I had to make money. So I went on signing my stuff Ann Lisle, Olivette, A. A. Waterbury and The Girl Reporter and interviewing stars in theater dressing rooms and criminals in prison cells.

Because of the way I handled a certain story, the astute editor who had given me my start sent for me and told me he was now ready to give me my big chance. One of the paper's important features, which had been a big "circulation puller" and had brought in an average of two hundred letters a week, was down to a puny thirty or forty responses. "You have a wonderful mother. Her daughter ought to be able to be Big Sister to the world," the great A.B. said, measuring me with his ice-blue eyes. "Go home to Boston for the summer and get her to teach you how to be a Delphic oracle."

My twentieth-century Don Juan did not approve of the plan and did not want a fiancée who let her work and her love for her parents send her off on a project which did not center around him. So he took back his ring, and I went home to learn from Mother how to give advice to the lovelorn. The weekly mail was sent after me, and she taught me how to handle it compassionately and with the understanding that "There, but for the grace of God, go I." Before my return to New York in the fall, I was getting more than a hundred letters a week, and I had learned to look on the work as a form of social service and to be proud to do it, proud of the perspective I could offer those who did not have a mother like mine to steady them.

That was a happy time. It came to a tragic end just after I signed an excellent contract with the feature syndicate which was then handling my work. The day I sold my first short story to *Cosmopolitan* and wrote to tell mother that my second story was going to buy her a little car, she died in her sleep.

On the day of the funeral I stood beside my broken, but somehow dauntless, father and watched the sobbing processional of those who had come to bid farewell to Mother in her coffin. Among them were the needy for whom she had found opportunity, the wayward girls she had set on the right path, and the slum children for whom she had established seven Sunday schools where they might learn to keep both their hands and their souls clean. Churches of various denominations housed those undenominational services rent free. The teachers were volunteers—students from Harvard and Wellesley. My valiant mother had superintended all seven schools. Her work had supported them as it had supported Father and me. Standing by her coffin, I vowed to see Father through because she had loved him.

When the funeral ordeal of pride and anguish was over, there was another ordeal to face. The prominent physician Father had summoned to take care of Mother in her sudden illness came to tell me he was haunted by the conviction that she might have pulled through if he had given her a stimulant instead of a sedative.

"But she was in such terrible pain," he said, groaning. "I couldn't stand by and watch that splendid woman suffer without trying to ease her torment. I decided she should have her night's rest and that the examination and diagnosis must wait till morning. I wanted to make it easier for her. You understand, don't you?"

I understood that the good doctor hoped to find peace by confessing his blunder. But he had shriven himself at heavy cost to me.

I had not known peace, I had not slept without sedatives since the day I learned that my mother might be alive except for a well-intentioned mistake. My success had turned into another irony, because it had come too late for Mother.

And now even success was going to be taken from me.

On that grim March morning, when I sat on a bench in Central Park reviewing all the twists and turns of my resentful and bitter young life, a famous diagnostician, who expected a royal fee for pronouncing my doom, had declared that if I went on using my right hand, my arm would soon be paralyzed.

For years specialists had been warning me that the acute pain and distorting swelling, to which my right hand was subject at increasingly brief intervals, were due to a rare and incurable form of neuritis. They all agreed that the condition would get steadily worse unless I stopped using my right arm. But I could not stop. I had to earn a living. I had to make a home for my father. I had to produce five thousand words of copy six days a week. I could not manage five hundred words a day without using my right hand. I could not use a pen or pencil with my left hand—it could not be taught to write or even to scrawl fast enough to keep up with the flow of ideas I had to get down on paper. I could not dictate my stuff because I grew shy at the sound of my own voice, and ideas stopped flowing. And even a typewriter demands the use of two hands.

Before long I'd have to stop writing Ann Lisle's "Snap Shots" and "When a Girl Marries." I'd have to give up Olivette's fashion column. Lilian Lauferty couldn't go on with the short stories which were selling to *Redbook* as well as to *Cosmopolitan.* All this was bad enough, but what really mattered was that I could no longer give advice to the lovelorn. I would not be a celebrity after I handed back the mantle of Beatrice Fairfax, which I had been wearing like a splendid borrowed ermine coat! And what would become of the thousands who had learned to write to the column with the confidence Arthur Brisbane had foreseen when he declared that Mother's daughter ought to be able to Big Sister the world? How would they fare if the department were turned over to someone to whom it would be nothing more than a "circulation puller"?

My own problem was as devastating as any that had ever come to me in one of the five hundred letters a week which was my average mail. I didn't know the answer to this problem; I didn't believe there was an answer.

For a frantic moment I tried to offer myself a perspective such as I would have offered someone else in a situation like it: There is a way out, and if you try hard enough, you will find it. Be brave. Milton wrote gloriously and *he* was blind. Have courage and recall what magnificent symphonies Beethoven composed even though he could not hear one note of his music.

But I could not make myself listen or heed. I did not want to go on with life on its sadistic terms. Soon I would be no good to myself or anybody else; my father would be better off without me. If I were not here to clutter things up, one of his rich sisters would feel obliged to make herself responsible for him.

I got up from the bench then and began stumbling down a path that led to the lake in the park. I could not bear any more; I had a right to find an escape from the pain in my arm, the loneliness in my heart and the resentment clouding my mind. I was conscious of the cold menace of the overcast sky and the stark nakedness of the March trees. I did not see the faint promise of the winter buds or the hint of blue behind the scudding clouds.

I went forward implacably. There was a sudden sharp turn in the path, and as I rounded it a dazzling brightness shone in my eyes and a yellow banner waved before them. Then the sun broke through the clouds and lighted the mass of shining golden stars that covered a Forsythia bush just come into lovely tender bloom.

Outside the compass of that moment, only a few seconds before, all the trees and bushes had looked angular and lifeless in the muted light of the dark morning. Now spring was coming back to the world, and I had seen the magic of rebirth.

I think I too was reborn in the moment when I beheld the golden glory of that Forsythia bush. I looked at it and knew that God was in this place. And I heard a voice saying, "I am the resurrection and the life."

Today I know that voice came from my own uplifted consciousness. Perhaps I knew it then.

Nothing in my tangible material existence had changed; but in the moment when I beheld the "burning bush" and felt the miracle of spring's return to the world my concept of life began to change. I was ready to go on with my work. I was not afraid of today's pain or of what might lie beyond today. The words of the famous diagnostician had lost their power to alarm me. I had become aware of another power. And I had a message to deliver.

It would be glorious to share the message of the golden bough with the hundreds who needed it. I must remind the lovelorn, the frustrated, the weary, the hopeless that spring always comes back to the barren world and banishes the darkness of winter from bush and tree and lonely heart. The voice which said, "I am the resurrection and the life," had not spoken for me alone.

Within the hour I sat at my desk and began the day's editorial. It was a two-column piece on immortality. If my right arm ached, I did not know it.

Some weeks later the magazine page editor laid the proofs of the next day's release before me. There, featured at the top of the page, was my story of what the return of spring to a tired world implies. It carried the by-line of Beatrice Fairfax.

"Of course, it's too late to do anything about it now," the editor said in a flat dusty voice. "Tomorrow more than a hundred papers all over the country will be carrying your comments on spring and Forsythia bushes and Life Eternal in the space dedicated 'Advice to the Lovelorn.' I'll never know how that piece got by me; but I do know that when the big chief sees it, we will be looking for jobs—you and I both—dear Beatrice."

Before the next day was over it was evident that our jobs were quite secure. Telephone messages and telegrams began pouring in shortly after the paper hit the streets. The article on immortality brought in something like a thousand responses from bereaved, bewildered, suffering people who had found a reason for hope in the message of the Forsythia bush. Those letters bore witness to the fact that spring can indeed blossom again in the heart which had seemed frozen into the pattern of winter and despair and death.

More than thirty years have passed since that bleak day when I was as desperate and defeated as some of you who read this may think you are today. They have been good years, productive years, years of growth.

I am still typing with both hands, and they have produced four novels, many short stories and magazine pieces, and numerous radio shows, among them "Big Sister," the story of a woman who wanted to Big Sister the world. I gave up newspaper work when I was married, not because I could not use my two hands, but because there was other work for them—the work of a home.

My father lived to be almost ninety and had fifteen years of health and happiness. He found a devoted son when I found the right man. The twinkle came back to Father's eye, and one day when all three of us had been to the ball game he said, "Don't we have fun since we married Jimmy Wolfe!"

My husband and I had a silver wedding anniversary in 1949, and we thought it worth celebrating!

The message of the Forsythia bush has stayed with me. That first whispering of faith has evolved with the philosophy of the years; so today I speak with a sense of authority when I declare that "the kingdom of God is within you." No matter how long you (like the "me" of that gray March morning) have been in bondage to fear and suffering and uncertainty, God is indeed a "very present help in time of trouble" to those who turn to Him with all their hearts.

It is not because I *believe* this, but because I *know* it and have proved it over and over again that I have been willing to tear this chapter out of my heart and set it at the beginning of my book.

Now you know the reason of the hope that is in me and something of the reason why I believe that I can show you the path to hope and confidence and joy.

PART I

Inspiration

Learn to Think Constructively

I

SHADOW IN THE SUN

My care is like my shadow in the sun—
Follows me flying—flies when I pursue it.

—QUEEN ELIZABETH OF ENGLAND,
"On the Departure of Alençon"

THE events of your day take on the shape and color of your thinking. You cannot achieve more than you can conceive. The steamboat and the airplane had to be thought out before they could be worked out. And thought produces moods as well as things. Neither gaiety nor gloom is an entity, an object existing somewhere outside the individual who feels happy or sad. Emotions express the state of mind which has set them in operation.

It is your response to stimuli, to what you call circumstances, which makes them challenges or commands, which leads to victory or defeat. What you and I accept as real in our experience becomes established fact to you and me and operates as a condition with which we must deal.

One midsummer morning three oddly assorted companions set off for a holiday in the Bernese Oberland.

The three—banker, lawyer and musician—had often climbed the Swiss Alps together and always with the sturdy, seasoned guide Franzel, in whom they had great confidence. They began this trip in high spirits, and before nightfall of their first day they reached a mountain hut from which they could look down on the Lake of Thun, glowing with splashes of amethyst, ruby and flame spilled down from the sunset clouds. They exulted in the view, in their sense of triumphant well-being and in the hearty food with which the hut was stocked. They made a banquet of sausage, cheese, rolls and chocolate, and then they curled up on the floor in their blankets for a deeper and more satisfying sleep than all the feather beds in Bern could provide.

It was still dark when Franzel's yodeling woke them. They had a sumptuous breakfast duplicating last night's dinner, stuffed their pockets with rolls and bars of chocolate, and set off briskly in the morning mist. As they climbed they watched eagerly for the sun to fling its banners of rose and amber across the peaks of the distant ranges. But the mist deepened from pearl gray to slate, its frayed curtain dropped down over their narrowing horizon, and there was no sign of the dawn.

The climbers ascended into a silence remote from the world, and soon they began to feel remote from one another, with nothing to link them but the rope.

Toward noon flurries of snow came swirling out of the sullen sky. Before long the flakes gave way to needles of hail which stung the cheeks of the climbers and pried at their eyeballs with avid fingers. But they went on doggedly, knowing they must make the next hut before the dense black of a starless night shut down.

They crept up a perpendicular of ice into which the guide had to cut steps for them. First the musician, then the lawyer and finally the banker, who was the best climber of the three and so had to take the dangerous end position on the rope, climbed slowly upward. They skirted a bastion of rock so steep that no foothold could be cut into it. At last they caught up with Franzel, who was waiting for them on a narrow ledge jutting out from a wall of rock they could sense rather than discern. The guide told them gruffly that they had better rest here and eat their rolls while he went ahead to look for some sign of the next hut, which should be only a few meters away.

After the mist had swallowed Franzel, the banker began to curse and the lawyer to mutter. The musician tried to whistle, but his cold lips would not pucker.

The holiday was becoming an ordeal. The three men huddled together in silence, waiting for a shrill yodel or a brisk bark of command from Franzel to bid them advance. They had been friends for years; but now they found nothing to say to one another, and the world around them was silent. The stars had withdrawn, and there was nothing but the glint of the hail to stab the premature dark.

The musician felt the rope between him and Franzel slacken and jerk, go taut and sag. He grimly dug his pick into the path and said nothing, but as he braced his body, the banker cursed again and then said that if the guide was to lose his footing and slip over the rim of the shelf they were on without cutting the rope, they'd all go down to perdition.

"Cut the rope!" the lawyer moaned. "Cut it now while there's time! Franzel can take care of himself. Why should all of us be lost?"

"The rope is slack now," the musician said. "I think he's on his way back to us. And don't forget that we'd be lost in any case without a guide."

Then Franzel came creeping out of the mist; but he brought no comfort with him. He acknowledged that he had never before come through the mountains by this way and did not know where they were. What he knew was that the ledge broke off sharply less than fifty meters ahead of them, and that there was a bottomless pit below them. If it hadn't been for the rope, if the pickax with which he was groping ahead hadn't held him back, he probably would have gone down into that pit.

Franzel said he'd been able to make sure what lay beyond the ledge because he'd done some measuring with three big white stones left by an avalanche which had broken off the shelf. He'd hurled the first stone straight ahead because he'd thought they might be on the lip of a crevasse he could span with his rope. But when the rock didn't thud on the other side he knew, since he was a distance thrower, the space was too wide to bridge. Then he made a second test. This time he hurled the stone downward and listened for the clatter of rock on rock. When he heard nothing he sent the third stone after the second. But there was no sound. No sound at all. The stone had hit bottom so far below that the noise of it couldn't reach his ears. He knew he was on the edge of a bottomless abyss.

All through that long night of sleet and wind and biting cold, four half-frozen men huddled together on the perilous shelf against the brooding mountain. Franzel yodeled now and then, and he begged the musician to sing. They must all keep awake, for if one of them were to sleep and stir uneasily in his dreams, they might all go sliding down into the abyss. Tomorrow, God willing, Franzel declared, he would lead them back to safety. Tonight they must watch with him or there would be no tomorrow.

In the faint gray of another misty dawn the guide began working his way toward the end of the ledge, and the singer crept after him, winking the frozen rime from his lashes and peering about in the haze with eyes afraid to pierce it and see what lay below.

Then there was a sudden shifting of tensions, and the musician felt a sense of balancing in space and knew that the rope had been cut behind him. He braced his body and shouted a warning to Franzel. The mountain mist was lifting; but he had just lost two friends, and there was a mist in his eyes as he crouched on the rim of the abyss with death in the depths below and treachery behind him. But the world grew shining and beautiful as veil after veil of gray nothingness curled back and the peaks of a distant range began to glow with the light of dawn.

The light brought revelation.

Only a few feet below the narrow ledge where the four frightened men had huddled together against the freezing cold of a long grim night a meadow of alpine grass spread wide and green. A man could jump in safety to that thick green carpet. It would have made a soft bed for lost travelers. And down in the meadow, half hidden by the cushioning grass which had muffled their fall, lay three white stones, the stones Franzel had hurled, the stones which had sent no sound of rock on rock back to the guide's anxious ears.

There was no abyss.

For many of us the path of experience leads, not once but again and again, to the brink of what a terrified imagination interprets as a bottomless abyss. The evidence we grope for and find seems to support our grim conclusions. Often, as on that morning in the snowy Alps, there is a green meadow where circumstance has testified to a bottomless pit.

If you are one of those whose thought patterns have involved them in a life of dark forebodings, if you are given to accepting terrifying suggestions which have doomed you to long nights of fear on the brink of one abyss after another, surely you must be longing for mental security, surely you must be seeking a new approach to life.

So consider this simple fact: You do not offer your hospitality to human guests you dislike or distrust. You do not of your own free choice invite undesirables into your home. Occasionally you may consider it expedient and even compulsory to ask relatives you find uncongenial to visit you for a week end. But no one can be forced to entertain ideas which make him miserable. Then, why not refuse to accept unwelcome suggestions into your mental home?

You can shut hostile fancies out of consciousness by closing the door of your imagination against what you do not want to nurture there. You have the latent ability to direct your mental process in the way you want it to go. Cultivate that ability!

You, like all thinking beings, can focus your attention on what you want to perceive, understand, develop and bring out or REAL-ize in life.

From the time when the earliest books of the Bible were set down onto parchment scrolls prophets and seers have been assuring mankind that there is a way of escape from the land of Egyptian tyranny, from the bondage of fear. The way to freedom is indicated by a single sentence from the Book of Job: "Acquaint now thyself with him, and be at peace: thereby good shall come unto thee."

To familiarize yourself with the constructive, the creative, the positive forces of life and to recognize that they are the expressions of that great over-all good we call God is to begin to REAL-ize them.

When you and I were children we were taught that there is a "Father of all, who is above all, and through all, and in you all." (Ephesians 4:6.) Some of us have never been quite convinced that there is a God and that He is our Father, the parent mind from which intelligence derives. Some of us need to be reminded of it from time to time.

This book is a reminder.

2

AS A MAN THINKS

With the God of heaven it is all one, to deliver with a great multitude, or a small company. For the victory of battle standeth not in the multitude of an host: but strength cometh from heaven.

—The Apocrypha, I Maccabees 3:18, 19

A few years ago a certain narrow city street was filled with the harsh stridency of drilling machines. The din lasted for days. During that period a well-known humanitarian, whose office windows opened out over the babel, had to prepare a complicated report and to document it with material from his files. So he was at his desk every day, and he worked without comment or complaint. But his secretary tingled with a compound of resentment and compassion because her chief had to be subjected to such a nerve-racking ordeal.

On the afternoon when the construction job was at last completed she rushed into her employer's private office and announced, "Now you can work in peace! All that horrible noise is ended."

"What noise?" he asked gently.

During the week of bedlam he had been undisturbed. He had work to do, and he had given himself over to that work. So he had never been consciously aware of the din. His nerves had not been racked. He had kept his thoughts on a level where irritation, annoyance and self-pity could not intrude. The cacophony, like the storm in a well-known hymn, had roared *without him!*

Anyone who earnestly desires to cultivate the habit can learn to keep himself undisturbed by conditions beyond his control and with which there is no point in getting involved. Constructive thought is selective thought, directed thought.

Thinking is not a haphazard thing, uncontrolled like daydreaming. It is at once a science and an art. To think constructively requires a recognition of the source of thought and also a technique of efficiency. All technique results from practice. A talent for music is not enough to make a great flutist or cellist. It takes work to make a master. Even genius needs developing and directing.

When a man has learned to focus his attention, to control his mental process, and to consider what is going on around him dispassionately, constructively and without yielding to dark forebodings about the possible abyss ahead of him, he is ready to make practical use of his resources and to harness his thinking and make it work for him.

Ideas must be activated in order to be expressed; they have to be expressed in order to produce results and win rewards. It takes directed thinking as well as constructive thinking to make a happy, orderly and successful life.

Man is his own builder. An individual's reaction to a situation, a mechanism or an idea is bound to affect his relation to it. A family feud, a power motor which everyone in the family wants and nobody in the family is willing to operate, the symphony which the genius in the family believes he could compose if he were relieved of all responsibility present widely different problems in family relationship. But one law is applicable to all three problems and will solve each of them. To heal a breach in human relations, to learn to handle a complicated mechanism, to develop an inspiration are alike impossible until constructive thought is brought to bear on them. Mere physical effort will not solve anything, accomplish anything or originate anything.

The only way any of us can successfully deal with a challenging situation is to think his way out. The only way anyone can develop a congenial situation is to think his way into it. "For as he thinketh in his heart, so is he," says Proverbs 23:7. And what this "he"—this man or woman—does, how his business, human relations and spiritual growth are developed and fostered stems directly from his own consciousness.

Each of us begins to free himself from limitations when he discovers the high level to which it is possible to lift his mental processes.

Joseph was thrown into a pit, sold into bondage, traduced and imprisoned, but he never thought on the level of his enemies. He thought above the thwarting situation, whatever it was, and so lifted himself above it and out of it!

After a man has learned how to harness his thinking and direct it, he uncovers potentialities he may never have dreamed he possessed. But as long as anyone has a limited sense of power and expects a limited portion of good, how is he to advance beyond those self-imposed limits?

The man who sees everything he longs to achieve or possess as "out of bounds" becomes a cynic, a drone or a criminal.

An engineer in the field of industrial research recently told a group of his fellow engineers that in order to develop better products there is one preliminary necessity: an enlarged thought about what it is possible to produce. To illustrate his point he said that when the Diesel motor was first being developed for use on railways railroad men demanded an engine which would run a hundred thousand miles without overhauling. Later on, some of them began to demand more, and as the goal was advanced results began to exceed the original estimates of what the engine could do. The standard was then set even higher, and the time came when the engine could run four hundred thousand miles without overhauling.

The speaker added that he was now convinced an engine would run "as long as the designer thought it could." Then he made the amazing statement that it might run even longer than that if "anyone became fully convinced that it ought to!"

Henri Bergson declared that an intelligent human carries within himself the wherewithal to surpass himself. What is this "wherewithal" but man's conscious relationship to a creative intelligence which does not know limitation? And what use can anyone make of this mental equipment unless he is aware of possessing it?

During the First World War a number of famous artists were stranded in Switzerland. Most of them had been stars in Germany, popular favorites of opera or stage or screen who had become public idols. But on August 1 they became enemy aliens and were glad to escape from Germany with nothing but what they wore and had been able to stuff in their pockets or hide in the linings of their shoes. They made for the haven of neutral Switzerland where they came very near starvation, since the little state which gave them refuge had nothing to offer travelers bent on earning money instead of spending it.

Eventually the former headliners found work and one another. As soon as the war was over they also found a manager who helped them arrange a revue *intime,* and then booked them for a world tour.

The revue, with its folk songs and dances and chorus of former stars, was a success in London and Paris, and when it reached New York it settled down for a run which promised to restore the fortunes of the still-forlorn group. Every afternoon the expatriates from a dozen continental countries huddled together in the "foreign city" whose language only a few of them could understand. They always talked of the happy time when their world tour would be completed, the war forgotten, Europe restored to its former beauty and order, and when everyone could go back to his homeland.

After a few weeks a young singer from the Baltic began to tire of all the nostalgia for yesterday's lands and customs. So he started wandering off by himself to investigate the customs of the country where he was living.

One September afternoon he was walking down Broadway toward the famous opera house, which was the goal of his dreams, when he saw a great crowd milling around in Times Square. It was far too early for the subway rush, with which he was already familiar; and nobody was showing any desire to go anyhere, as he had thought New Yorkers were always wanting to do. He crossed the street to investigate and found that everyone was watching a long bulletin board on which numbers and letters were flashing. Now and then people would roar with delight and jump up and down and slap one another on the back; but the words they were shouting were not included in his small English vocabulary. He asked a timid question. Half a dozen people began trying to explain. What emerged from the bystanders' limited French and German and Italian and his equally limited English was that this was the first game of the world series and that everyone was watching the score.

A world tour he understood. A world series was quite foreign to his thinking. That a crowd of people should be standing in the heart of a busy city watching numbers flash on a scoreboard was also foreign. But he reminded himself that he was just one person, and the crowd numbered hundreds. This, it seemed, was America. He would stay and find out more about it. After a while some strange osmosis of excitement began communicating itself to the man from the Baltic States. Before going to his dressing room that night he bought a ticket to the next New York game of the world series and had a fairly clear idea of how to get to the field where it would be played.

His Old World friends laughed at him. Why did he want to see a ball game? Playing with balls was for children. Why should a grown man pay to watch children play ball? All right then, so the players were men! Didn't that prove that all Americans were children? He was no child, his friends reminded him; he was a cultured, sophisticated European artist. Why should he spend all that money for a ticket to a *ball game?*

The young adventurer said he did not see why a sport which amused so many Americans should bore him. As a matter of fact, he had amused himself very well watching the numbers flash on and off in Times Square. So it would doubtless prove even more interesting to watch men instead of numbers. "If I want to find out, I must go and see," he said. "Already I think it will be good to sit in the open looking at something that happens before my eyes instead of sitting in a room looking back at a past which is forever gone for all of us."

A few months later the revue was stranded in a town out in what the ball-game addict had learned to call "the sticks." The show was too *intime,* too continental and too slow-paced for general popularity.

The young singer, who had been interested in finding out how the United States played, had very little difficulty in adapting himself to its working ways. Before long he had found an American booking agent, and the agent had found him a job as soloist in a Broadway motion-picture palace. An attainable goal had been reached: The singer was now identified with an American institution. In the movie house he learned more about the ways of the country and began to feel that he was an "American in the making." He determined that he would be an American citizen someday, an "American by choice."

Two years later he reached the goal toward which he had been striding on that day when he stopped to learn why hundreds of people were milling around Times Square. He became a member of the Metropolitan Opera Company.

There were many fine artists in the revue from which our singer emerged. Only a small percentage of them widened their horizons to include the scope of customs, manners and mores of the country they were mentally *passing through.* Those who were engaged with the past would not acknowledge that there was no return to it. Some could not accommodate themselves to the idea of starting over again; some rebelled at being unknown in a strange land; some despaired of being able to adapt themselves and their artistic standards to what they called the commercialism of the United States. Most of them became waiters or entertainers in small cafés where their own languages were spoken.

Those who were prepared to adjust themselves to the New World were able to make a place in it. One of the group is a noted scientist, another is a recognized physician, a third is a successful dance director, a fourth the owner of a fleet of taxicabs, and a fifth has a delightful antique shop. Each emerged in his own way, in his own time, but not until he was ready to push back his mental frontiers and venture beyond the limited horizon of his immediate vision.

Progress demands that we enlarge our frames of reference and encompass new references in our frame of vision. A limited sense of things produces a limited crop of things.

All pioneers must vanquish their own hesitancies, traditions, superstitions and taboos built up by human fear of the unexplored. Each day presents some challenge of unknown frontiers. Human progress is based on a long series of adaptations to the unknown and unproved. There is no refuge in the past. There is no holding back today and its demands for directed thought, wisdom to recognize inspiration and courage to follow the light.

The spiritually enlightened man is aware that the abyss will probably turn out to be a grassy plateau. He recalls how often, as he has advanced toward a distant mountain, it has leveled down into a gentle slope.

When men first awaken to the magnificence latent

in them, they may "see through a glass darkly," may catch no more than a glimpse of the immeasurable possibilities in the realm of thought, of mind itself. Men develop their power not by bravado but by the humble recognition that there is a reservoir of power on which to draw. The way to implement ability is to use it, to train it, and to employ it continuously in full confidence that it will not fail.

There is a sound basis for such confidence. What is called "second wind" is the reserve of human strength, the stamina with which the coward and the quitter never make acquaintance. But when men drive themselves beyond that first sense of exhaustion—or despair or maladjustment—which claims that they have spent their last flicker of energy, their last ounce of strength, their determination to go on helps them find the wherewithal, the awareness of a boundless source of power. Whoever draws on this source taps the infinite reserves of spiritual power, of divine intelligence, of infinite good. And so he proves the presence and potency and wisdom of God.

3

SEEK AFTER WISDOM

Some trust in chariots, and some in horses: but we will remember the name of the Lord our God.

—PSALMS 20:7

THERE are skeptics who insist that everything is the result of chance. Some of them waver to the extent of acknowledging a force they call antichance. But even the great intellectual who, with a show of authority, denies God cannot disprove Him.

The positive sense of Deity had to be formulated before there could be a contrary sense. There had to be something to deny before anyone could start claiming that there was nothing. The negative is impossible and even unthinkable until there is a positive for it to dispute.

"We are born to inquire after truth; it belongs to a greater power to possess it," Montaigne wrote in the sixteenth century. The search has gone on all through the ages. It starts always with a desire for understanding, for "more light"; it is generally based on the conviction that there is a basic reality and that it is worth discovering.

It requires faith to believe in anything at all! And faith

demands accepting something one may not be able to prove absolutely. There is still a limited field of proved fact.

In an arresting little volume called *Does God Exist?* Dr. A. E. Taylor, late professor of Moral Philosophy at Edinburgh University, defines faith as "assent to something which you cannot prove beyond all possibility of being wrong."

Dr. Taylor establishes his point by a direct and cogent argument along lines similar to these: Practically anyone can demonstrate that two plus two equals four. As I write this statement I am definitely aware of my fingers operating on the typewriter keys. I am an actual witness to the process by which these words are being put on paper. When they appear on the white sheets, I know how they got there. But I cannot witness with equal conviction the words Abraham Lincoln spoke in his Gettysburg Address. I was not there. I did not hear his voice. Still I have full faith that Lincoln wrote the words of that immortal speech and delivered it. Though I cannot actually testify or bear witness, I assent to this idea, because there is a record of the Gettysburg Address and a historical report about the circumstances connected with its delivery.

You and I would never engage in trying to set aside the vast number of historical facts of which we have no first-hand knowledge and of which there is no one alive to bear witness. We believe that George Washington crossed the Delaware on a certain night and with certain results. Our belief is based on the fact that we have read about the event in history and have seen indications of what came of it. We cannot deny history without challenging much of what has been recorded as part of the world's events.

Now, to go all the way with our adaptation of Dr. Taylor's wonderful argument, it is perfectly obvious that there is very little about which any of us has an assurance to compare with our firsthand knowledge of our hands on typewriter keys, or on steering wheels or in soapsuds! We go through life taking things on faith. *Then why not take God on faith?* As soon as we do this, as soon as we postulate the Deity of which we have so much evidence and claim that God *is,* we find more and more evidence to support our faith.

Here is the brief chronicle of an experience which recently befell a skeptic who was forever declaring that religious beliefs were absurd and full of fallacies, and that the religious were emotional children lacking in logic and maturity of thought. He claimed that the mature mind must worship culture and that there was no other god worth serving. He insisted that no intelligent human being could believe more than he could prove, that no man could prove the existence of a supreme power and surely not the existence of a benignant power bent on blessing and protecting all creation.

This amiable atheist contended that he could think his way out of any undesirable situation in which he might find himself involved. He challenged anyone to pray his way out of actual difficulties. His god, he never hesitated to make clear, was pure reason. He summed it all up like this: Men make for themselves a deity endowed with the qualities they most admire. Whether you call this an idol or an anthropomorphic god does not change the fact that it is a man-made deity and no more than a figment of man's imagination. "No idols for me!" our friend declaimed. "And call him the Devil or call him God, your Supreme Providence is an idol."

In the late fall this man went to a deserted beach resort on a remote part of the Maine coast. He wanted solitude so he could write a book which required great concentration. All the cottages near the house a friend was lending him were closed for the winter. This eminently suited the author who felt a great need to be uninterrupted while he thought out some of the more abstruse problems having to do with his subject: the relation of superstition to religion. He meant to deal with this theme conclusively and devastatingly in his book.

At the end of a month his ideas had refused to "jell." Though the scholar did not know it, it is not an easy thing to defy the Creator in the face of a magnificent view of creation; from the knoll where his cottage was set there was a superb view of the turbulent ocean. Sometimes the visitor felt overwhelmed, but whether by his topic, the loneliness of his days or the melancholy of autumn he did not know. One morning he woke and saw a mellow haze and knew that Indian summer had come to warm the grim season; so he decided that this was a fine chance to tone himself up with a little swim down in the harbor below the house.

He swam toward the south, sedulously avoiding the rocky ledges and jutting promontory at the northern end of his beach. When he began to tire he turned over on his back and floated in the buoyant salt water, and the chapter which had been eluding him began to shape up in his mind. He was so absorbed in his meditations that he did not concern himself with the time of day, nor feel the strong ebb tide until he realized that he had drifted far out of his intended course. The swirling undertow did not frighten him. It stimulated him. He thought he would enjoy an argument with the waves and the tide, so he swung over and began to swim toward the now distant shore. He exulted in his long, powerful stroke and his tussle with the surging water, until he realized that it was not getting him anywhere and that the shore was farther distant than it had been a few minutes ago. He put all he had into his kick, but he made no headway.

He was not accustomed to being afraid, but when his legs knotted with cramps and waves from a hidden ledge broke over his head, he began to feel helpless and alone in a dreary waste. And he found himself shivering with a coldness that seemed to come from within rather than from the now icy water.

Then he heard somebody's voice shouting in that vast

nothingness: "Help! Hi there! Help! I'm drowning! Save me!"

In a moment of detachment he recognized that it was actually he who was screaming to cold and inimical space and to the elements which had ganged up on him. He laughed at his absurdity and tasted the salt in his tight throat.

Then he shouted again, only half aware that he was calling on a power beyond anything he had ever accepted or acknowledged as power. "God, help me! I'm about done for. God! Save me, or I perish," his panicky voice pleaded, and the part of him that was still sane wondered what he was quoting.

The only thing he knew clearly and without any sense of division in his thought was that there was nothing he could do to fight the merciless sea. It was not aware of him. He was no more than a log bobbing on the waves, which might carry it inexorably to the other side of the world. He could not make his way back to his snug little harbor and safety. He could not do anything. Everything he had trusted had failed him. Then he called out quietly and deliberately: "God, it's up to you. I put myself in your hands."

He felt very peaceful then. He was all through battling the implacable tide. He lay on his back smiling up at the sky and waiting for help to come.

The current swept him out beyond the farthermost point of the bleak northerly promontory he had feared and avoided. He watched incuriously as he went past it. Then the eddying water sucked him around this point of danger and into another little harbor fully as snug and peaceful as the one he had thought his only haven.

He did not write his book on the relation between religion and superstition. He says he doesn't quite know why; perhaps it's because he's turned a bit soft, sentimental, superstitious or what have you. But just the same he can't write his blast at religion and religion's God as long as he's not certain whether he was saved that day by chance or by design. He smiles wryly when he says he can't repudiate his own miracle; and because of it he's half convinced that there is a cause, a motivation at work in the world, and that it is at the root of all that it is intellectually impossible to explain—or explain away.

"I don't *know,*" he says. But he is not yet humble enough to acknowledge that there is a primal cause.

This primal cause is what most of us call God. And many of us have found that when we turn to basic cause, and away from the depths of our preoccupation with material despair or material arrogance, this causative power operates in behalf of the one who invokes it.

We have already seen that we develop a talent, that we cultivate an ability, by exercising it. We would never think of denying that we learn to play the violin by playing the violin, not by playing canasta or tennis. We cultivate our gifts by apprenticing ourselves to the art forms in which we long to excel. But we often let life itself be wasted without making any intelligent effort to learn how to live.

There is no need to take life as it comes if what comes is not welcome. Instead of striving to be a good sport about unhappy experiences, why not prepare the way for happy ones? Why not work to approach the art and science of living at least as intelligently as we would work to develop a talent for dancing or painting or playing the piano?

Several years ago a young woman, to whose experience I can bear witness, was sent to a private hospital. Her physician warned her that she had a double heart murmur and that the least exertion might cost her life. The doctors at the sanitarium bore him out, and she was ordered to rest in a high bed with two special nurses assigned to keep her absolutely quiet. The patient, whom we shall call Martha since she was a Martha by nature, could not rest because of her fierce worry over what all this was going to cost and what would happen to her and her dependents when her savings were used up.

At the end of a week Martha's condition had not improved, and she was so desperate that she had no welcome for her first visitor. It was an aunt whose circumstances were so modest that Martha was astonished at her gift of a beautifully boxed, leather-bound volume. When Martha discovered that it was a Bible translated into modern English, she was annoyed and was tempted to tell Aunt Sally to take it back and get some good novels in its place.

But something, perhaps a flicker of courtesy greater than her petulance, stopped her. Then Aunt Sally insisted on reading aloud from the book, and Martha was definitely enraged at her aunt's calm assumption that anything the Bible said, in modern or Elizabethan English, was going to have a healing effect on heart valves that didn't work properly.

When the visitor's hour was up she begged her niece to keep her thoughts filled with the message in Psalm 138:8. "That will help you," Aunt Sally said confidently. "And tomorrow we'll find another message."

"Miss Devens from my office is coming to visit me tomorrow," Martha said stiffly. Aunt Sally wasn't offended; she said she could come the day after tomorrow.

After her aunt was gone Martha went through a series of reactions. I'm too young to die, but here I lie . . . done for, she thought resentfully, and my favorite aunt, the only relative I have in this part of the world, doesn't see how grave the situation is or offer me a little human sympathy. Instead, she acts as if a pep talk is all I need! She can't afford ten-dollar presents and that handsome book looks as if it cost all of that. I don't rate more than half a dozen carnations. . . . I'm being a meanie. Aunt Sally thinks she brought me something anybody would love to own. But why didn't she leave it on my bed? Why did she put it 'way over on my night table if she wants me to study that verse she's so sold on? I wish I could remember how it goes. She acted as if it were a magic formula. How did it begin?

Martha could not remember. So she sat up in bed cautiously and reached for the book, The Holy Bible: A New Translation, by James Moffatt. When she had managed to get hold of it, her heart began to pound, and she lay back on her pillows terrified because even this little exertion had been too much for her. But after a minute or two her curiosity overcame her fear, and she opened the book and searched for Psalm 138. She skimmed through it hastily until she came to the eighth verse, the last verse:

> The Eternal intervenes on my behalf:
> Eternal One, thy kindness never fails,
> Thou wilt not drop the work thou hast begun.

A wave of bitterness surged over her. "Thy kindness never fails," she protested. But here I am snuffed out, and what's to become of my folks when I'm dead?

After a moment of still fury Martha flung the book across the room. Then she lay still, engulfed in misery and pain. She refused to eat the creamed chicken and rice on her supper tray; so the friendly young nurse said orange juice with an egg whipped up in it might slip down better, and she trotted off to fetch it.

But when Martha was alone again she began to cry. Her misery had taken a new turn. She was ashamed of herself for being so ungracious to Aunt Sally. She was worried about the book. The force with which she had hurled it might have crumpled its gold-edged leaves or broken its binding. She lifted her head and saw it sprawled in the shadows on the other side of the room. She was ashamed of the way she had treated the handsome volume. Some people called the Bible "the Good Book"; she could not leave it lying face down on the floor.

Martha tossed back the covers of the bed from which she was not supposed to move. When she crept back into the high bed again, she did not feel any the worse for her exertion, for what she called her "rescue mission."

I wonder if God has begun to take an interest in my case? she asked herself ironically when she realized that her heart wasn't thudding. She liked her mood. Irony was better than whimpering; evidently she was getting hold of herself, preparing to be a good sport about her fate. Anyway, now that she had recovered the book she might as well read that verse again. It had an interesting rhythm. She learned it by heart before she went to sleep. She slept that night without a sedative.

The next day she asked her nurse if the hospital had a library and if the library had a King James Version of the Bible. When the book was brought to her she looked at once for what she had begun to think of as her verse and not Aunt Sally's any longer. The way it read in the King James Bible was:

> The Lord will perfect that which concerneth me: thy mercy, O Lord, endureth for ever; forsake not the works of thine own hands.

It seemed to Martha that "forsake not the works of thine own hands" was a desperate petition to a faraway power, the only kind of prayer she had ever known how to make. But "thou wilt not drop the work thou hast begun" was a confident declaration; it brought God near, within her reach.

Then it came to her that when she was a little girl and afraid she had only needed to put her hand in her mother's hand, and she was not frightened any longer. She had been sure that her mother would take care of her.

She read the verse again, pondering every word. If the Lord would not drop the work He had begun, if God was intervening in her behalf, why didn't she just put her hand in his and relax?

Martha got so interested in her train of thought, in the ideas that were coming to her, that she forgot her body. When Aunt Sally came the next afternoon, Martha asked if she knew any other Psalms as interesting as the one hundred and thirty-eighth. Aunt Sally picked up the King James, without seeming surprised to find it there, and read Psalm 91. This time Martha listened eagerly.

> He that dwelleth in the secret place of the most High shall abide under the shadow of the Almighty.

As she heard the words of the Psalm, the girl in the hospital bed felt a sense of peace, an awareness of being in a secret place where she was being helped and protected. She felt a great longing to abide there.

When Martha told her aunt about it, Sally said, "You

can. It's mental. Thoughts can't think you; you've got to think them. Think good thoughts, Martha."

Within a week one doctor said Martha was making a marvelous recovery, and another said there must have been a mistake in the diagnosis. In a fortnight she was dismissed from the hospital. Before the month was out she was back at her work. Today she is a well, happy, successful and deeply spiritual woman whose confidence continues to abide in the "secret place of the most High."

A true understanding of God has practical as well as spiritual aspects. A great editor once told a struggling young author that she would do better work if she got up from her knees and sat down at her typewriter. She saw the point and stopped thinking of writing as a great art and far beyond her humble little self. She elevated her concept of herself, and in time she came to see that self as one of the manifold expressions of the creative intelligence which operates through many channels and in varied forms. Then she was able to get up from her knees, from awe-struck idol worship, and sit down at her typewriter to express her inspired ideas.

Reverence for Deity and the gifts of God means that gratitude is taking the place of fear. Understanding of the source of all intelligence and power gives man an awareness of his ability for free, joyous activity, and shows him the folly of groping in the dark of superstition and uncertainty and the halfhearted effort which comes of them.

Moses, one of the first of the world's great leaders of men, gave his followers a magnificent assurance before he left them: "The eternal God is thy refuge, and underneath are the everlasting arms. . . ."

Centuries later, as he came to his disciples across a stormy sea, Jesus called to them: "it is I; be not afraid." The "I" of spiritual consciousness to which he then referred was the son or reflection of God to whom he was always referring.

The assurance of power, the Christ or truth, still comes to us across the stormy waves of human experience. The voice of spiritual understanding is speaking to us today. In these pages I shall set down the record of many who have heard that voice and have been directed by it in circumstances where nothing but a clear awareness of God's presence and power and good will to man could have saved them from what appeared to be inevitable destruction. Through understanding faith in good these men found the "wherewithal to surpass themselves." They heard the still small voice of truth.

All who would hear this voice must learn to listen.

4

THE BUSINESS OF LIVING

Man is his own star . . .

—JOHN FLETCHER, "Honest Man's Fortune"

THE business of living is at once a science and an art. There is no lasting and satisfying success for anyone except as a result of his own disciplined thinking.

Carved in letters of stone above the entrance to Town Hall in New York City are words whose significance is for all time: "You shall know the truth and the truth shall make you free."

The truth, the enlightenment which releases man from bondage to darkness, is revealed through culture and education. We have all come to recognize that education is more than a process of study and training or even of learning the material facts about the phenomena of the external world. It is not enough to master a number of theories and formulas; one must know how to make use of what one knows.

And culture is gracious. Without the graces of spirit the educated man may be a boor and a bore.

Erudition is never enough. Real education brings out

a man's awareness of his own capacities and of his ability to draw on them; culture makes him respectful of another man's learning and confident of his own knowledge. The freedom which follows such intelligent self-confidence is the light shining in darkness and dissipating the fog which hides truth from ignorance.

But human wisdom lacks completeness unless it includes an inspired confidence in God. Without an awareness of a purposive cause or mind the world is a place of grim uncertainty and the conditions with which man must deal are bewildering and menacing. But darkness has never been able to persist when the light was turned on.

Truth is the light in which man beholds his relationship to the purposive, causative, creative power we call God. So when human thought becomes aware of its source and of its relation to the basic intelligence of the universe, it is free.

When Maurice Maeterlinck declared "None but myself shall I meet on the highway of Fate" he was saying that man is the creator of his own destiny. But this does not leave God out of the reckoning. What it actually indicates is that in the degree of our mental alliance with the constructive forces of good, or of our submission to the destructive forces of evil, we design the pattern of our days. This is a poetic and unforgettable way of reminding us that we are never justified in blaming failure on a malign fate. We are free to choose our goals and work our way toward them.

What you and I acknowledge as law becomes the law

of our being. There is no escaping this fact, and we must state it and restate it to ourselves until we have incorporated it into our thinking. *We shall REAL-ize in our experience that which we claim as the normal expression of our being.* Our harvest of success or failure, of sickness or health, of joy or misery results from the seeds we have sown in our own field of thought and endeavor.

Failure, like success, is a concept before it is an accomplishment. We invite misery and frustration by opening the doors of consciousness to them.

An elderly man in Indiana owned a horse which went right on winning harness races long after its trotting days were supposed to be over. An officious acquaintance asked the owner how he dared to drive such an old horse and if he didn't think it risky for a veteran like him to go careening around the track in a flimsy little sulky.

The veteran laughed. "My horse wins," he said, "because he doesn't know when he's licked. I don't aim to get fainthearted before he does. No horse is going to shame me."

The man who magnifies his problem minimizes his ability to cope with it. Ambition and the desire for achievement and the courage to ignore limitations or laugh at them are wonderful equipment for any race.

If you, like a great many of us, are given to taking what you call your personal dignity too seriously, think of the elderly jockey and his elderly horse and smile away your own uncertainties and insecurities and resentments.

Recently an outstandingly successful career woman

acknowledged publicly that she was by no means the heroic and dramatic figure her admirers claimed.

"I never had to climb icy pinnacles, nor to ford swollen torrents," she said to the audience who had assembled to see her receive a distinguished award. "I did not scramble up to my goal on bleeding feet, nor tear my hands on the brambles through which I had to beat my way. Once or twice the going was pretty rough, but whenever I got sorry for myself and got misty-eyed over my difficulties, I couldn't see to pick my way. So the going got still rougher! Then I began to figure that it was stupid to build up my molehills into mountains . . . because I had to climb them.

"When I saw that clearly, I began to get myself in hand. I stopped standing and shuddering on the edge of little streams and telling myself they were floods I'd have to swim. I looked for a bridge or a ford instead. And sometimes I found I could jump over what I'd been almost self-mesmerized into seeing as a torrent. Then I got the habit of listening when I told myself not to make it so tough for me. From then on the going got easier and easier. Not that it's too smooth even yet. But I've learned to laugh at the frightened little self that tries to say, 'I'm you, Carlotta!'

"Now I'm telling you—and reminding myself to listen to what I'm saying—that anybody can conquer fear by breaking the habit of building up the opposition until it looks bigger than Goliath. And I'm going to give you the Bible verse that actually is my formula for success. So here it is, and remember I didn't make it up. I just make use of it. 'O magnify the Lord with me, and let us exalt his name together.' That's all any of us needs to do: magnify good; lift up your ideas about the nature of good and you'll stop being scared to death of the bogeyman who's bound to get you if you don't watch out and see that he's nothing but a silly scarecrow."

It is not easy to organize and discipline thought, to train it to expect good and to deny the power of evil suggestions or appearances. To do this through mere personal endeavor would be a formidable task. But throughout the ages there have been great teachers and great leaders who recognized that " . . . there is a spirit in man: and the inspiration of the Almighty giveth them understanding." (Job 32:8.) This understanding has always made the business of living more efficient and more secure and therefore more joyous and satisfying.

More than twenty-five centuries ago the prophet Jeremiah wrote these words of promise: "I the Lord search the heart . . . even to give every man according to his ways, and according to the fruit of his doings." Jeremiah spoke as if he were convinced he knew the mind of God and could interpret it. He did not question his ability to lift his consciousness to the summit of understanding where he could actually hear the word of God. In some degree all the spiritual leaders whose words have come down to us across the years have identified their thinking with a great reservoir of thought which they named God.

When Jesus said, "I and my Father are one," he was

fully identifying his real being, his true selfhood, his consciousness of life with the searching mind, the rewarding wisdom which Jeremiah had to some extent recognized.

Abraham, Moses, Isaiah and a host of inspired thinkers of varied countries, languages and races recognized that God is potent and near at hand, and that man is not shut off from His presence but can learn and do the will of God. Christ Jesus carried this awareness to its logical conclusion when he declared his oneness or "at-one-ment" with his Father, God.

Isaiah wrote:

> Thou wilt keep him in perfect peace, whose mind is stayed on thee: because he trusteth in thee.
>
> Trust ye in the Lord for ever: for in the LORD JEHOVAH is everlasting strength. . . .

Turn to infinite wisdom and you will see that God expresses Himself in and as mind. So He is not a God afar off but is as near as your own thinking acknowledges Him to be, as near as your confident receptivity brings His power and wisdom.

The ability to recognize a sustaining, governing mind, or basic cause, and to invoke its power is latent in every thinking man or woman.

The Psalmist said:

> How precious also are thy thoughts unto me, O God! how great is the sum of them!

Anyone can cultivate the great and rewarding spiritual ability to "think God's thoughts after Him."

Begin by refusing to extend your mental hospitality to the suggestions of doubt, uncertainty, suspicion, hate, resentment, envy, jealousy and self-pity. Don't dally with them. Slam the door in the face of every suggestion of injustice or frustration which tries to invade your house of life, your consciousness; start inviting desirable mental guests. Cultivate joy, love, activity, generosity of viewpoint and the widening spiritual vision which flows from them.

Take your stand for the qualities of thought you wish to REAL-ize as facts of experience. Try honestly and earnestly for just one day to "dwell in the secret place of the most High." You will find it pleasant there and will probably want to stay on for another day—and then for another! Persist in this stand for good; invite it into your consciousness and expect to have your invitation accepted. After a while the *method* of thought you are practicing will become a *habit* of thought. You will find it a very satisfactory habit!

Try to gear whatever you do and say to the concept of yourself as man in full possession of God-given dominion over everything with which you have to deal. While you maintain this sense of identification with good, this "I-and-my-Father-are-one" consciousness, you will find yourself in possession of a capacity and an authority beyond anything of which you have ever before been aware.

"It's all right if it works," says the pragmatist. But even

if men had no higher aim than efficiency, there would be comfort and satisfaction in proving that it does work to trust good. There is no denying the old saying: "What thou seest, that thou beest." So for each individual who refuses to parley with the suggestion that there is any power which can successfully oppose good there is an increased conviction that evil is not an entity and has no power.

Evil is negation. It is nothing but the denial of good. No one can be compelled to deny his friends and give aid and comfort to his enemies unless he gives consent and so becomes a party to his own destruction. If you were totally out of sympathy with the thesis that to support evil in thought is to invite it into experience, you would not have read to this point.

Actually it is no great trick to set the machinery of frustration and failure to work. No one ever wrote a book, composed a symphony, built a bridge or a business, or worked out an Einstein theory by thinking he couldn't. Negative thinking weighs men down with self-imposed handicaps. Defeat stems from lack of confidence in ability to succeed. However this basic truth is expressed the fact of it remains: *No man achieves in spite of himself but because of himself and his conscious, affirmative stand on the side of the angels of dominion and power.*

In Lewis Carroll's *Through the Looking Glass* the Red Queen tells Alice that one must run very fast to stay where one already is. And, as in most of the delightful Carroll nonsense, there is a great deal of sense in the Red

Queen's statement. The architect whose plans do not keep pace with modern requirements will find himself losing ground to the forward-looking, *now*-minded men who are moving ahead with the times. It is axiomatic that a successful career, like a successful business, demands an awareness of what is going on in the contemporary world.

A merchant who has unlimited credit at his bank is not afraid to expand his business. Then surely the man who grasps the fact that he has access to the infinite resources of mind has even greater reason for expanding his thought.

In the realm of spiritual awareness there is no bottomless abyss, no incurable disease, no unendurable sorrow, no unattainable goal. Now, as in the days of Moses and Jesus, truth is at hand to lead men out of bondage and make them free. This truth is as near to each one of us as he is prepared to acknowledge.

The state of human thinking which goes about the business of living with full faith in the source of its being and a confident awareness of its relationship to creative mind cannot fail to REAL-ize its heritage of power.

5

BEFORE THEY CALL

And it shall come to pass, that before they call, I will answer; and while they are yet speaking, I will hear.

—ISAIAH 65:24

"PRAYER is man's greatest means for tapping the infinite resources of God." These are not the words of an ordained minister of the Gospel. They are the declaration of J. Edgar Hoover of the FBI as quoted in the *Baptist Observer* of Indianapolis, Indiana.

To accept the magnificent concept that prayer enables us to tap the infinite resources of God means to abandon the notion that prayer is a method of persuasion, of prevailing on God to bestow some blessing which is being blindly or capriciously withheld.

We have all heard prayers which sounded as if they were based on the idea of recommending to the Creator of the universe some improvements in His plan. Real prayer is not an attempt to inform God of anything; its purpose is to inform ourselves of what God has in store for those who love Him, of the constructive goodness which is God, of what the Psalmist meant when he prayed:

> Open thou mine eyes, that I may behold wondrous things out of thy law.

Prayer tranquilizes human thought so it may perceive what already exists in the spiritual realm of mind's creating. Prayer changes human concepts and reveals that God is eternal good which does not have to be changed but accepted.

> Trust in the Lord with all thine heart; and lean not unto thine own understanding.
>
> In all thy ways acknowledge him, and he shall direct thy paths.

These two verses from Proverbs clearly indicate that prayer is not petition but communion. To declare good sincerely and understandingly is to come into unity with it.

The prayer that avails does not ask for material changes in an external universe but for inner vision, an awareness of the beauty and perfection already existent in the world as God created it.

> 'Tis heaven alone that is given away,
> 'Tis only God may be had for the asking . . .

We moderns may consider James Russell Lowell's *The Vision of Sir Launfal* dated, but its message is still abreast of the times if not ahead of them. The poem tells the universal truth of the everlasting quest for achievement, of how cringing and plotting along self-seeking human lines may defeat its own purpose, and of how seemingly ultimate defeat can be turned into victory.

When the frustrated and aging Sir Launfal came sadly home from the dream quest, he had nothing but a crust of bread to show for his efforts. But at the end of his tired journey he found what he had missed in his arrogant youth; for when he reached out to bestow a blessing instead of seeking one, when he was ready to share his crust with a leper, he found the Christ.

Real prayer includes the vision that can pierce the fog of human misperception and behold the truth of spiritual creation.

Once upon a time a ship carrying passengers to Italy was caught in a tempest and driven from its course. One man, a prisoner who was being taken to Rome to appear before Caesar, warned against the danger of continuing the voyage, but the owner of the vessel was scornful of his advice. The prisoner struggled against his resentment at the stubborn master of the ship, who was subjecting some three hundred people to danger on a storm-tossed sea. When the prisoner's own thought was quiet he was able to look away from the monstrous waves, to ignore the howling wind and to turn completely to God in prayer. After he had gained his full sense of unity with his Maker, an angel—or inspiration—came to him and filled his thought with wisdom and compassion.

When the ship was grounded on a reef and broken, the prisoner discovered a way of escape which had not been evident to the experienced mariners on board the wreck. This time his suggestions for charting a course to safety were not rejected. Perhaps it was because he spoke with true authority now, the authority of dominion over himself and his human emotions. Perhaps it was because the peril from the mountainous waves was so great.

Everyone on board the doomed ship escaped to a rocky island where the barbarous people were kind to the voyagers. It proved a safe harbor, as the prisoner, the apostle Paul, had foretold. He had prayed effectively in what seemed a hopeless situation. His prayer had availed in that it made him quiet and receptive enough to perceive the way of escape.

Now, just in case you regard this account of answered prayer, given in the twenty-seventh and twenty-eighth chapters of the Book of Acts, as a fanciful tale, a Bible story that has nothing to do with life as we know it, how about this more recent "miracle" as related by a young Marine who experienced it during the Second World War? (He told it to a group of us who were working to help the Treasury Department publicize and promote the bond drives.)

While on the Murmansk run this boy's ship was lost from its convoy during the cold darkness of a winter's night. Shortly before midnight the ship was torpedoed and so badly damaged that it began to list at once. The wireless was put out of commission, and it was not possible to send an S O S.

The situation appeared hopeless on board that sinking

troopship in enemy-infested waters. But our Marine and his buddy began to pray aloud. They had learned in Sunday school that God is the loving Father, the protecting Savior, the ever-available helper of all who turn to Him. So they prayed in the confident belief that the Father hears His children when they call. They sang hymns, they assured each other and the few who would listen that "underneath are the everlasting arms," and that help is always available for those who claim God's protection and expect to see it manifested.

Even when they found themselves clinging to spars in the icy sea, these boys held to their awareness that God is a God at hand; and they continued to declare that the All-Knowing understood their need and how to meet it. Presently a lifeboat came along, and they were pulled on board into temporary refuge. Now the two Marines had definite and tangible proof that the power they were invoking was operating. They thanked God and went on declaring His presence so that all on board the lifeboat might hear. As they sent out their S O S reverently and confidently, the men around them stopped cursing and groaning; and before long everyone in the little craft was singing hymns.

Shortly after midnight of that same night, one of the escort ships in the convoy turned back in the darkness to look for stragglers from the formation. For some time the captain of this ship had been fighting what seemed like an insane impulse toward a dangerous infraction of orders. But he was so strongly impelled to turn back that he finally told some of his officers of his conviction that they must alter their course. Then it developed that a number of them shared what a junior lieutenant called a "hunch" that there was need of them somewhere in the wake of the wide-spaced transports of their convoy.

In the gray light before dawn this escort ship found hundreds of half-frozen men afloat in lifeboats or clinging to wreckage in the water. The torpedoed ship had not been able to send an S O S, but the spiritual S O S had been received. Our two Marines were among the thankful survivors rescued through what most of them insisted was a miracle.

Many of us know of similar episodes. All of us can recall how Captain Rickenbacker and his companions survived long days of exposure and thirst in a wilderness of uncharted waters. The captain's faith in the Bible and its promises sustained them when everything else had failed them.

Many such experiences have been related and recorded; and none of them are miracles. They are proofs of the normal sequence of cause and effect. They resulted from the confident faith of some happy few who had heard and had believed that man is not separate from the creative mind he was made to express.

Whether on a remote mountain peak, in the seemingly impenetrable jungle or on a turbulent sea, man is never lost merely because his formidable and alien surroundings indicate that he is. Man is lost when he loses hope, when he gives consent to calamity. When and as man lifts his thought and his awareness of being to conscious unity with that wisdom and power which are ever-present to sustain him, the inspirations of intelligence prepare a table in his wilderness and lead him to it.

The power on which Paul relied almost two thousand years ago, the understanding which made those Marines on the Murmansk run certain of a God at hand are available to you and to me today. If we desire to be protected and guarded and guided by that power, we must invoke it. We must deliberately and confidently establish our contact with the omnipresence of God, good. We have our part to play in gaining our own salvation.

When man is consciously aware of the availability of good, he keeps in communication with God. Then he learns that "I and my Father are one" is not a formula but the truth of spiritual being and that men can still ally themselves with it. Jesus never said a word to indicate that the ability to utilize man's relationship to his Maker was something which belonged to him exclusively. He declared cogently that power belongs to God; he proved he could manifest this power and explained that it was natural to him because he understood that he was the son or expression of God's mind. He also said that greater works should be done in times to come. If we believe him (or Moses before him), we cannot deny that the mind on which he relied and through which he expressed the eternal Christ, or truth, is available today for all who invoke eternal mind confidently, reverently, humbly and with understanding. In the degree of our acceptance of our established relationship to the source of all life, to the extent of our identification with our Creator, we can prove faith's practical value.

"Let this mind be in you, which was also in Christ Jesus," Paul told the Philippians. But in order to obey Paul's charge and to "let" our blessings unfold we have to put aside scoffing intellectualism and arrogant self-will and permit our thinking to be an agency for wisdom. It is really not too difficult, and it is well worth a try! Innumerable people have found it so.

We communicate with God through prayer. Prayer puts us under God's law; it sets the good will that is God's will in operation in our lives.

We pray in order to lift our sense of existence out of its preoccupation with the confusion and struggle with which human planning is involved. So don't try to furnish Deity with a road map to your chosen goal; and don't be too stubborn about that goal. Wisdom may have something better in store for you than you have imagined. None of us is wise enough, or farsighted enough, or well enough informed to be certain about the best route out of our wilderness and into our Promised Land.

Many of us are not ready or willing to turn to God in humble expectant prayer until we have lost faith in any other hope of solving our problems. We pray because we have learned in a hard school of failure, disappointment and misery that no material prop, however strong and sturdy it may look, can be relied on as a bulwark against hurricane or flood, or as a staff to support us when an avalanche sweeps toward us. But even if we have refused to turn to the spirit of God until everything else has failed, we are never put off with a stern edict that it is too late.

"Now is the day of salvation," and it is always *now.* Mind is always operating, and there is never any obstacle outside of stubborn individual consciousness that can keep us from communicating with it.

There is nothing theoretical or fanciful or transcendental about invoking God. We merely tune in on supreme wisdom, and since it is omnipresent we find it when we seek it. Actually our alliance with God is already established. All we need to do about it is to become aware of it and claim it. As we acknowledge and invoke the established law of good, it begins to operate in our lives and to govern our experience.

The power of faith has been proved again and again in my own experience. If the Bible account of Paul's escape from shipwreck and a poisonous asp on the Island of Malta seems nothing but ancient history to you, if the account of the rescue on the Murmansk run also seems remote and something which could never happen to you, how about something which took place on an automobile trip through New England? I can bear witness to it, because I was there when it happened.

It was late in August, and my husband and I were hurrying back from a vacation in the mountains in order to rush to New York for an important business meeting. We took a recommended short cut through a New Hampshire mountain pass and found ourselves on a narrow road thick with heavy clay. After an optimistic mile we faced the fact that we were in a wilderness. There were no houses in that desolation, there were no side roads leading out of it and no turns. A granite slope rose sharply at the right, and at the left a forest of treetops marched down into a distant valley.

My husband's hands grew tense and white on the wheel as he tried to hold the car to the narrow, deep-rutted track. Suddenly the path dipped, the machine got out of control and began to slither off to the left where scrub was taking the place of treetops. We could see the sheer drop into the ravine. As our car slid toward the brink of the slope, I heard myself calling out, "God!"

That was a prayer, a call for help. My inmost self was invoking a great and good friend in the confident assurance that He would hear and take care of us. It was as if I were a child calling on a beloved parent to come and save us from a bad dream.

"God!" I called again, reverently.

The driver's hands jerked at the steering wheel, and the car lurched to a stop. It hung over the edge of the slope with a boulder wedged between its front wheels and its body tilted crazily but not overturned. Almost as if he were observing the situation instead of experiencing it my husband said, "He heard you!"

We sat very still for a while. Perhaps we were afraid to move. I do not know. I only know that we had just been held back on the brink of a ravine. Finally we managed to climb out of the right side of the car. We were unharmed, untouched, and deeply, reverently grateful.

We set off at once to find a way out of our wilderness. After floundering ahead through the slippery ruts for perhaps half a mile, we reached a clearing where the slope on the left began leveling off into what seemed to be a meadow. In the far distance, on the other side of the field, we could see a moving something which looked like a matchbox on wheels. Convinced that there was help on that other road, if only he could reach it, my husband clambered down the hillside and started on his mission. Presently I saw him jumping from hummock to hummock and realized that our meadow was a marsh.

Then I turned my thought earnestly to the power that had directed our wheels to the shelter of that barrier rock on the brink of the ravine. I did my best to claim and REAL-ize that the wisdom which had guided those hands on the steering wheel would direct the feet out of the marsh. I declared fervently and with growing confidence that the power which had just operated in our behalf was still in operation. I filled my consciousness with the beauty of a verse from Psalm 62:

> My soul, wait thou only upon God; for my expectation is from him.

I clung to that and waited. . . . In time a rescue squad appeared—my husband and two helpers.

The "matchbox" had turned out to be a jeep carrying two young government surveyors sent out in advance of a crew coming to build a new highway through that region. The sturdy surveyors had heavy-duty chains in their jeep and were able to pull our car off the rock.

They hauled us down the long stretch of corduroy that lay between us and a crossroad, and then they sent us on to what they assured us was the best repair shop for miles around.

While he was working on the car, the mechanic who owned the shop delivered a little monologue.

"It's a mercy you folks didn't go crashing down into the glen when you skidded in that ornery mudtrack some darn fool told you to cut through," he said. "I'll bet that there boulder that stopped you is the only sizable rock along that whole ten-mile stretch. It's a miracle you come up with them surveyors! Ain't nobody used that road for close to a year. 'Twasn't ever fit for anything but a logging road. But the real miracle, for my money, is how you ever drove the three miles from where them government boys turned you loose. It sure beats all how you could keep coming with the front axle bent till them front wheels of yours was toeing in so far they darn near ran across each other's tracks!"

But neither of us has ever thought of that experience as a miracle. We know our safety was the answer to prayer. It was the proof that God *is,* and that He is ready to answer before we call.

6

THE WORLD'S BEST SELLER

The English Bible,—a book which, if everything else in our language should perish, would alone suffice to show the whole extent of its beauty and power.

—THOMAS BABINGTON MACAULAY,
"On John Dryden"

TO THOSE not fully persuaded that there is a God it seems that believers assume the existence of the Deity without being able to prove it. Recently a puzzled and reluctant skeptic demanded of a great and tolerant religious leader: "But don't you have to base all your teachings on a hypothesis you can't prove? Don't you have to start all your theories and teachings by postulating God?"

"No, you have to start by being aware of Him," the teacher answered.

The Bible is of inestimable service to mankind, because it develops that awareness.

All through a sleepless Christmas Eve, Kay Smedley had faced the facts about herself and had found them grim. She was approaching forty, and she had come to the end of her human resources. A few years before she had been a successful businesswoman, one of New York's high-salaried stylists. Yesterday she had borrowed the money to buy Christmas dinner for her brother Bill's two little orphans.

Self-pity mingled with self-condemnation as Kay recalled the day when she had felt that she had owed it to her dignity to walk out of a fifteen-thousand-dollar-a-year job because a younger woman had been promoted over her head. For two years after that she had held out for a position in her income bracket. Now it was beginning to look as if the fashion world did not have a place for her in any income bracket.

Kay was aware that she had once had a reputation for being difficult and even snobbish, though decidedly glamorous. Now she was merely shabby! She could no longer manage even a fortnightly visit to the beauty parlor; her clothes were becoming dated; and she, too, was dated and quite forgotten. She shivered with the misery of being nobody; but the final misery of her night-before-Christmas vigil was the realization that Katie and William would not be having a turkey dinner on Christmas Day if a stodgy old friend of Bill's had not lent her the money to pay for it.

At dawn the once-pampered Miss Smedley crept out of the bedroom she had to share with five-year-old Katie and went to the kitchen to make the chestnut stuffing William told her they always had at home.

As she worked she stared with aversion at the big bird

she had bought with her final delusion of grandeur and the first money she had ever cadged. Hideous word! More hideous fact; but this and other facts must be faced. She should have saved some of those twenty dollars to buy presents for Katie and William, whose empty stockings dangled long and thin from the mantelpiece where optimistic William had hung them last night before going to bed on the living-room couch.

Kay finished peeling the chestnuts and went to work on the onions. Naturally they made her cry. Having accounted to herself for her tears, she reminded herself that she had always been inventive and that she was bound to dig up something to fill those stockings.

When the turkey was ready for the oven, she tiptoed back to the bedroom where Katie was still asleep and began a muted search of the bureau drawers. She found a gay ribbon and a colorful handkerchief, a plaid silk change purse and a pincushion that would do nicely for a little girl. But she had nothing for a little boy. Then she recalled the book in which Mr. Holden had passed her the twenty-dollar bill yesterday. He had muttered something about its being a Christmas greeting, a volume recently brought out by a publisher whose advertising he handled. Kay had thought Mr. Holden an old fuddy-duddy for being so shy about handing money to a woman and a sanctimonious hymn singer for thinking she would be interested in a collection of quotations from the Bible. But it was a handsome little booklet; it would do nicely for stocking-stuffing. William had a present.

Kay sat down at her desk to inscribe the flyleaf, and the leaves fell open to a section marked "Proverbs." Her scorn abated a little when she saw the illuminated capitals. She turned the page and admired the handsome block letters. The letters formed themselves into words, and they too were beautiful:

> Trust in the Lord with all thine heart; and lean not unto thine own understanding.
>
> In all thy ways acknowledge him, and he shall direct thy paths.

She liked the rhythm of the words. She read them again, and they began to sing in her head. They sounded like a carol written for this moment and for her.

Courage, Kay, she thought. "Trust in the Lord with all thine heart; and lean not unto thine own understanding." That's vaguely familiar. Sounds like something I've heard before and liked. . . . Wait, this is it: "O rest in the Lord . . . wait patiently for him . . . and he will give thee thy heart's desire." The song swelled; it was an oratorio now—Mendelssohn's *Elijah*—and beautiful, beautiful beyond anything she had ever heard. It was unendurably beautiful!

Kay ran out to the kitchen, the only room where there was no sleeping child to be disturbed by her tears. She sat down at the kitchen table and put her head in her arms and sobbed. She felt better after that. She remembered that she had a handsome red-leather pencil case someone had given her several Christmases ago. It had red and blue and green pencils in it. It was just the thing for a boy of seven. The place was filled with things that unspoiled, grateful children would like. Once upon a time she had put these trifles aside scornfully because nothing less than gold vanity cases and enamel cigarette boxes seemed worth the attention of Miss Smedley. Now she thanked God for the simple things that would fill those long thin stockings.

The children loved their presents and their dinner. They sang carols with Aunt Kay afterward, and they listened quietly while she hummed "O rest in the Lord." Just as she was beginning to wonder how she would keep them happy all during the afternoon the telephone rang. It was Mr. Holden saying he'd had too much Christmas goose at his club and needed exercise, and he wondered if she would lend Bill's youngsters to him for the afternoon.

After the three of them had set off in high spirits, Kay did the dishes to the accompaniment of the Bible verse which went right on singing in her heart. When her house was in order she sat down to put her thoughts in order. It was high time, she told herself, for Miss Kay Smedley to be realistic. She'd have to come down off her high horse and her income bracket. A woman who had two darling kids to support must have a job; people were always looking for cooks, and she would take a job as a cook if that was all she could get. But first she could try for a position as clerk in a budget shop or a bargain basement.

I won't let Katie and William down. And God won't let me down, she found herself thinking. She reached for the book of Bible quotations, and while she was reading its reassuring words the afternoon slipped gently past.

The sound of the doorbell woke her, and in came Katie and William dragging Mr. Holden with them and both talking at once as they tried to describe their good time—skating in Radio City and seeing the ice show and eating all the ice cream they could manage. After they had scampered off to get ready for bed, it occurred to Kay that Mr. Holden might like a bite of the turkey for which he had paid.

During that impromptu supper Kay discovered that Mr. Holden was a very definite individual and not the mere fuddy-duddy she had thought.

"I would never have dreamed of putting this up to the fabulous Miss Smedley if she hadn't come marching into my office two days ago," he said. "But I can lay a forty-dollar-a-week business offer on any woman's kitchen table. I know it's not what women of your caliber call a salary. I don't claim it's much of a wage. Half a dozen top-flight stylists have turned it down. I'm praying that you'll have the vision to take it, because you seem like the answer to prayer."

" 'In all thy ways acknowledge him, and he shall direct thy paths,' " Kay heard herself saying with a complete lack of business caution. "I found that in the book you gave me to cover up and gloss over the twenty-dollar loan. . . . I need a job, Mr. Holden. I hope this is one I can fill."

The job was one Kay could fill perfectly. Mr. Holden's clients wanted to start a chain of shops selling high-style dresses at the lowest possible price. They could figure their margin of profit, but they needed a fashion expert to select and perhaps design their merchandise. They had more ideas than capital and were going to start cautiously with only two or three links in the chain. The forty-dollar-a-week wage Mr. Holden offered Kay that Christmas Day was their top salary.

The links have expanded into a sturdy chain, and Kay Smedley earns a real salary now. She is back in her old income bracket, but the fabulous Miss Smedley, whose pride and arrogance blocked the path, is banished from Kay's life. She knows where to turn for understanding and who directs her path.

A few verses from Psalms and Proverbs were a life line to Kay.

The Bible when spiritually understood is a book of life to any who turn to it and study its inspired chronicle with confidence in the word of God.

The first translation, from Hebrew into Greek, of the earliest books of what we call the Old Testament was made when the Ptolemies were ruling Egypt. Since then the Old Testament has been translated from the original Hebrew and the New Testament from the original Greek into more than eleven hundred languages and dialects.

In 1950 the American Bible Society, founded in 1816, reported that a total of 395,365,426 Bibles, Testaments and "portions" had been distributed throughout the world. "The Good Book" has achieved a top circulation of twenty-five million copies in one year. The Bible societies of the world include organizations in Great Britain, Scotland, the Netherlands, Norway, Finland, Japan, China, India, Pakistan, Argentina and Brazil.

It is good to know something of the history of a book which has held the attention of mankind for many centuries and has survived the ages and the changes due to its experience at the hands of men. Scribes left out words here and there and differed over the meaning of a phrase now and then. Obscurities grew out of the misapprehensions and contentions of scribes and scholars.

In spite of human vagaries the essential meaning of *Ta Biblía* has persisted; and ever since copies of the Scriptures were first made available, men have striven to possess them, because men longed for the message, the word of truth. That message is set down in the first chapter of the first book of the Bible. It is woven through the writings of the Psalmists, prophets and apostles. Each writer of The Books, in his own generation and after the fashion of his own experience and philosophy, has witnessed the power and presence of God, the one God, and the perfectibility of man when man sees himself as God made him and sees him. In the words of Solomon (Proverbs) the message reads: "For as he thinketh in his heart, so is he. . . ." In the words of Jesus the word is: "The Father that dwelleth in me, he doeth the works." Solomon recognized the power of thought; Jesus understood the presence of mind. In the years between Isaiah and Jesus the minor prophets foretold the coming of the one who would clearly discern that the Father dwells in His creation and that man can claim his heritage when and as he recognizes it.

The Bible had an influence in English life long before the King James Version of 1611 was produced. In Saxon days Cædmon made a poetic version of the Scriptures; and "the venerable Bede" translated parts of *Ta Biblía* in the eighth century. In 1382 John Wycliffe made the first complete English translation from the Latin Vulgate. Every copy of the Wycliffe Bible had to be done by hand, and the demand for it was so great that it was impossible to find enough scribes to keep up with it. There is a well-authenticated tradition that a farmer bartered a whole load of hay for a few chapters of the Epistles of Saint Paul.

When the printing press made it possible for three thousand copies of William Tyndale's New Testament to be struck off, Tyndale had to flee from England to escape persecution for wanting to "give the Holy Book to the unholy." That was in 1525, and England did not have royal sanction for the reading of the Holy Writ until the King James Version was authorized and produced in 1611.

The Bible has survived because men have always felt the need of it and its message. It is a chronicle of all human experience. It covers such a wide field of history, adventure, drama, poetry, psychology and philosophy that it seems defensible to claim that nothing can happen to the man of today which does not have its parallel in the Bible. So if purpose, determination or sense of direction falters, men do well to seek inspiration and guidance from this record of life, this Holy Writ.

For those who read it with enlightened eyes the Bible furnishes convincing proof of the protection available to all who turn to it in full faith that there is a divine power and that it operates for the fulfilling of the law of justice and mercy and salvation, the law of good—God.

The might of divine power was claimed and proved three thousand years ago by Samuel, the last of the great judges, the prophet instrumental in establishing the kingdom of Israel. Samuel considered himself the servant of God. He believed in divine guidance. He had an unwavering faith in the power which had led his forefathers out of Egyptian bondage. He thought it reasonable to suppose that this power was still operative in the affairs of men and that the voice of wisdom could still be heard by the listening ear. He did not forget nor doubt the power to which he had dedicated himself in his youth. But the children of Israel forgot, and so they began to worship strange gods.

In a terrifying crisis of their ceaseless warfare with the Philistines, Israel put aside its images of Baalim and Ashtaroth and appealed to Samuel to intercede for them with his God. With one accord they promised to return to the worship of this God if Samuel could persuade his Deity to save them from the approaching enemy.

Samuel probably did not approve of their attempt to bargain with the Almighty, but he was too compassionate to condemn them; so he lifted his thought to commune with the power in which he had full confidence. While he was waiting for an inspired message to give to the children of Israel, a violent storm broke over the countryside. The rolling thunder terrified the Philistines; they fled in panic and the Israelites found courage to pursue the stampeding host and put it to rout. After the victory Samuel set up a memorial stone and made a declaration which challenges the wavering thought of every generation: "Hitherto hath the Lord helped us."

There are only seventeen verses in the seventh chapter of the First Book of Samuel, but they give an account of a pattern of behavior which appears again and again in recorded history. In days of prosperity men worship the products of their material success. The work of their own hands engages their attention, and all they seek is more of it! But when the Philistines of their day threaten attack and all their idols prove powerless to avert destruction men recall how they have been protected and led in other crises. Faintly, vaguely and perhaps without much hope they recall that "Hitherto hath the Lord helped us." They face the unchanging fact that possessions, whether objectified in the form of golden images of Baal and Astarte, or as pearl necklaces and Ming vases, are mere *things*. They recognize that idols cannot stand or walk or go, that inert masses of perishable matter (however beautiful or valuable) cannot guarantee security to their devotees nor stand between them and their enemies. When men come to the point where they have no other defense, they either turn to the inspiration of spirit for directing or perish of their own stubbornness.

A challenging paragraph called "Learn to Live" was printed a few years ago in the magazine of a great fraternal order. It recorded a list of contemporaries who had clung to the golden idols of their own creating and of how those idols had failed their makers. It told of a meeting of the world's most successful financiers shortly after the 1921 depression had set in. Among those who gathered to determine the course of the future were the president of the New York Stock Exchange, the Secretary of the Interior, Wall Street's most famous "bear," the president of the Bank for International Settlements, the head of the world's largest monopoly, the president of the world's largest independent steel company, and the outstanding wheat speculator of that period. One of those financial titans lived on borrowed money for the last five years of his life, another died insolvent and an expatriate, two went to prison, and three committed suicide.

At the end of the paragraph there were two lines of comment: "All of these men had learned how to make money; not one had learned how to live."

Every one of those titans came at last to a barren wilderness of defeat and despair because he had lost faith in himself and had no other faith to sustain him.

All through the ages the basic law of honest practice has had the power to enforce itself. Justice catches up with men at the pinnacle of success, just as it overtakes them in the valley of frustration. One brief line in the magnificent Psalm 91 declares: " . . . his truth shall be thy shield and buckler." Men are constantly proving the protection this fact affords and as constantly having lapses of memory in regard to it.

There is no doubt that some find little in the Bible but support for dogma and creed; they translate its words literally and are shackled by their own interpretation of what gives inspiration to the inspired. But the man of vision discerns that "the Good Book" is a guide to living and a torch to light the way.

There are hundreds of timeless stories in the Bible. We cannot invent any method of involving ourselves in a wilderness experience which was not anticipated by some Biblical character. And the way of escape was always the same; it was always the way of spiritual enlightenment and understanding and dauntless confidence in good.

So *Ta Biblía* have survived the ages because they reveal so much more than a chronicle of human events. They record how you and I may become increasingly aware of an ever-available life principle to whose wisdom we can turn in any emergency however dire it seems to be.

Every age has its atom bomb. The hordes of Genghis

Khan keep sweeping over the horizon and disappearing beyond it again. The instrument of destruction that looks so threatening is always deflected from its path and rendered impotent when a Moses or a Jesus is present to show men how to turn to the only real power and to bring the wisdom of "all-might," the Almighty God, to bear on the threat of physical might and destructive force.

Life has always been a challenge. Great wisdom is required to meet the challenge of today. It behooves us to remember that creative mind has always operated in behalf of those who invoked it with full confidence in the invincibility of its power. This is the basic theme of the book which can well be called the Holy Writ.

PART 2

Organization

Learn to Harness the Power Within You

7

"AND LET NONE OF YOU IMAGINE EVIL"

What can we know? or what can we discern,
When error chokes the windows of the mind?

—SIR JOHN DAVIES,
"The Vanity of Human Learning"

MOST of us have very little sales resistance. We buy advertised brands. We follow fashionable trends. We let ourselves be stampeded into the fear that encourages epidemics. In a season of double-breasted blue serge suits, how many of us buy three-button gray flannels? When a choice bit of gossip is going about, only a few ignore the temptation to prove they are "in the know" by adding their burning brands to the bonfire of scandal. There is a tendency among men to judge by appearances and condemn on hearsay evidence. Our communities are swept by epidemics of opinion, and they owe their scope to the consent of the misgoverned.

Recent experiments in psychosomatic medicine show that if a hypnotized patient is told that he is being given a drug with a stimulating effect but is instead given one with a soporific effect, his own expectation will keep him awake and make him lively. The result of the dose will be the one for which the patient has been prepared instead of the one the drug is generally expected to produce.

After making some investigation and laboratory experiments along this line, Professors Merle Lawrence of Princeton University and Adalbert Ames of Dartmouth found that what an individual sees when he looks at something depends less on what is actually present than on "the assumptions he makes when he looks."

Professor Lawrence is quoted as saying, "What we believe to be the 'real' physical world is only an 'assumptive' or 'form' world."

More than a century ago, in 1838, Thomas Carlyle wrote, and was quoting in his turn: "The eye of the intellect 'sees in all objects what it has brought with it the means of seeing.' "

Two thousand years ago Jesus told his disciples that he had to teach the multitude in parables "because they seeing see not; and hearing they hear not, neither do they understand." Jesus perceived the spiritual reality instead of the "assumptive" or "form" world, and our scientists and scholars are beginning to prove by experiment what he knew by inspiration. But we of today go right on making life difficult by our acceptance of what seems to be and is not. We have never recognized the enormous practical value of the spiritual teaching of the great Nazarene.

In the early days of the motion picture the pioneering

companies felt no need of going to Italy or to the coast of Africa for actual on-the-spot locations. The chateau on the Riviera, the Kentucky moonshiner's shack and the Eskimo's igloo were generally sets, and the three of them might stand side by side on a California or Flatbush lot. There was no need of traveling to authentic locations. The camera could do all that was required to beguile the eye of a public so entertainment-hungry it was self-induced to visualize cardboard as marble.

Pretense goes on at every level of human experience. This is acknowledged as dangerous when the make-believe of childhood is carried past adolescence and into the years of presumable maturity; for then it becomes the stultifying escape mechanism by which the physically adult can hide from the need of coping with reality and can avoid becoming mentally adult and accepting the responsibilities of maturity.

It is imperative for men to clear their vision, to look at and through life's presentations with an honest directness that cannot be tricked into accepting the papier-mâché set as a real structure with the dimensions of reality.

Many years ago a mysterious woman moved into a secluded house on the main residence street of a small Midwestern town. The neighbors went to call on the newcomer, but a dour and craggy maid came to the door and said her lady was not at home. To make the dismissal more emphatic, a dog barked from the shadows of the inhospitable hall.

Nobody from the house of growing mystery was seen on the streets, but sometimes passers-by caught glimpses of a veiled figure flitting about behind the high hedges; and they agreed that a small black animal was always at the woman's heels, but they could not agree whether it was a dog or a cat. Somebody said it was black and probably a cat since witches always had black cats. Somebody else reported that she often heard strange music coming from the house after midnight. Before long the town had a witch.

Children avoided her side of the street in daylight, and even grownups scurried by after nightfall.

One Sunday morning in early spring ten-year-old Linda was dispatched to her grandmother's house with some cinnamon buns her mother had made. It was only eight o'clock, and the little girl thought the witchwoman would be sleeping; so she did not cross the street to avoid the dark house. As she went hurrying by she smelled a perfume she loved. Inside the high hedge she glimpsed the first lilacs of the season, and the magic of their scent lured her into the witch's yard. She ran to bury her button nose in the rich fragrance, and after it was too late to escape she saw the witchwoman gliding toward her with a pair of enormous shears in her hand.

Linda stood rooted to the spot, and when she could not lift her feet she remembered the story about the girl who was changed into a laurel bush. She looked down at her feet apprehensively. But as soon as she saw her own Mary-

Anns instead of the roots she had half expected, she found a voice and called out, "Oh please, if you're going to turn me into a bush, make me a lilac!"

The witch laughed. It would have been a lovely laugh if it hadn't sounded dusty and as if it hadn't been used for a long time. Then she spoke in a voice so beautiful it made Linda think of the violin her father sometimes played. "So you love lilacs too," she said. "I want you to have some of mine. All you can carry." She brandished her big shears, but it was to snip off great plumes of lilac.

Then there was an excited barking, and an eager little black Scottie arrived and began sniffing at Linda, as if she were his idea of a lilac. Linda's feet came unrooted, and she stooped to pat the little fellow. Then she looked up to ask if she could give the doggie a bun and forgot all about her question when she saw the zigzag scar that covered one side of the lady's bare face and the dark blush spreading all over it. She knew at once why you didn't have to be a witch to wear veils all the time except early Sunday morning when everyone was supposed to be home in bed.

"But you're beautiful anyway," Linda said with a child's savage honesty. The lady put her hands over her face, and Linda saw that they too were scarred. The child asked God to tell her what to say, and words came and said themselves: "And your eyes are just the color of the purple lilacs at my granny's house. But hers aren't out yet. And I couldn't believe my nose when I smelled your lilacs. So I came in without being invited. I'm Linda Loring, and I hope you're not angry with me for coming into your yard. I don't want you to be angry because I like you so much, and I'd like to be friends."

"I like you too, Linda," said the lady. "I'm Mrs. Forrester, and I'm glad you came in. But I must run now; I've forgotten something. Please take all the lilacs you can carry. Take some for your granny too. And I'll ask you to come again someday . . . when I can."

The lovely dusty voice got all tangled up in a sob, and the lady ran to her house. Linda hoped she wasn't going for her veils but just for her handkerchief.

That afternoon Linda and her mother went to the house where the lilac bush was in bloom, and Mrs. Forrester opened the door for them.

Later, while the child and the Scottie romped together in the yard, Linda's wise mother put her arms around her little girl's new friend and said, "Tell me as much as you can trust me to know."

Then the woman, who had been regarded as a creature of ugly mystery, and even as a witch, sobbed out her story. She had tried in vain to save her little daughter's life in the fire which disfigured her own face and twisted her hands so badly that she could not go on with her career as a concert pianist. After a few months in a sanatorium she had come to her grandfather's old home to hide her damaged face and her broken heart.

"I was bitter and envious," she told Linda's mother, "when I saw other mothers with their little girls. And I died every time they turned their eyes away from me. But your little girl didn't turn away. She smiled at me and said my eyes were like purple lilacs. I ran into the house to hide my tears. . . . They were cleansing tears. They washed away my resentment. Then I started to wonder if other people beside Linda might find something to like in my poor face. And now here you are with your arms around me as if you didn't find me at all repulsive."

That is how a Midwestern town came near having a witch and got a wonderful piano teacher instead. The children all loved Mrs. Forrester. They couldn't agree whether her eyes were like the dark French lilacs in Linda's granny's yard or like the violets they found in the woods; but they agreed that her voice was like music. And the left side of her face was beautiful!

Not so long ago a group of people whose beliefs differed somewhat from those of their neighbors found themselves and their convictions threatened by a bill which was under consideration in the legislature of their state. The threatened minority sent a representative, Mr. Jones, to talk to Senator Smith, the author of the bill. Before Mr. Jones set off to see the senator, he was briefed about his opponent. He was warned that the man was as sly as a fox, that he was dedicated to his own career and convinced that he could best further it by serving "the vested interests" opposed to everything Mr. Jones and his friends represented.

The emissary, prepared for all the tricks the wily senator might use against him, set off for the state capital, but the fox eluded him, and the mission failed. The senator did all the talking and would not give Mr. Jones a chance to present his viewpoint or to say a word about the four freedoms and their application to the situation. When the interview was terminated, Mr. Jones started home to acknowledge that he had failed miserably.

He got into his car feeling chagrined over the way he had been outsmarted. Then he became self-righteous and indignant. But as the wheels of the car rolled along he began to recognize the age-old fact that hurt pride doesn't solve any problems and that he had been delegated to cope with a problem which menaced the principles of a group of fine people who had trusted him to work it out. Then Mr. Jones confessed to himself that he had made a tentative, halfhearted and slightly superior approach to the legislator, because he had been thinking of Smith as a tricky, double-crossing, double-talking fox. Suddenly he became aware that as long as he was seeing a fox in the senator's big swivel chair, he would have to deal with a tricky fox!

Then Mr. Jones turned his car around and drove back to the capital. Before the day was over he had another appointment with Senator Smith.

At the end of an enlightening two-way discussion, the senator said, "You're a reasonable man, Mr. Jones. I see your point of view, and although I don't share it, I respect it. Now I wonder whatever gave me the impression that you were a blustering Master of Hounds with your pack hot on my trail and that you'd ride me down if I didn't take mighty good care to elude you?"

"We both saw through a glass, darkly," Mr. Jones said. "Now we see face to face if not eye to eye."

The senator smiled and nodded. The two men shook hands. Then they worked out a modification of the bill effecting a compromise which was fair to everybody concerned.

The seemingly irreconcilable interests over which individuals, families, clans and nations wage mental war are very likely to be based and built on false assumptions, on misperceptions of the truth. The veiled lady was not a witch, and the senator was not a fox; but until those who misperceived them got a different angle and made an honest effort to see through the fog, the false concept appeared to be the true one.

When we misperceive or distort reality, it takes on the guise of our picturing; and unless we change our false concept, we have to deal with the pretense that is largely our own creation. When and as we recognize this truth, it will free us from false belief and enable us to discern the unchanged facts which were always there whether we saw them or not.

When and as we develop a sales resistance to evil and the rumor of evil, we make room in consciousness for good report and for growing awareness of our ability to "think God's thoughts after Him."

Behind the clouds of suspicion and fear and doubt which

operate maliciously to separate men of good will, the will of God is hidden from view. But it is there! It is visible, perceivable, when "the clouds of sense roll back and show the form divinely fair," as a well-known hymn puts it.

You and I and all the world need more of vision, more of perception, more of understanding and more of brotherly love. Then we shall see what *is* and not merely what *seems* to be.

For peace on earth we need to consider the words of the prophet Zechariah, who lived some five hundred years before the birth of Jesus, but who manifested the Christ spirit when he said: "And let none of you imagine evil in your hearts against his neighbor. . . ."

8

"GO INTO PARTNERSHIP WITH GOD"

But oars alone can ne'er prevail
To reach the distant coast;
The breath of heaven must swell the sail,
Or all the toil is lost.

—WILLIAM COWPER, "Human Frailty"

WHEN we begin to recognize universal intelligence as a basic fact of life, we start to express it in our individual lives. When we recognize that we include the qualities of creative mind in our real being and that wisdom and judgment are part of our natural equipment, we face the world with a confidence nothing else can give and nothing whatever can take away. Failure and success alike are contingent on ratifying our relationship to creative intelligence, on going into partnership with God.

A few years ago a group of prominent citizens gave a banquet in their flourishing southwestern city. More than a thousand people came to the dinner in honor of a man who had lived there obscurely for the first thirty years of his life. Now, at sixty, Richard Prentiss had become a national figure. Recently he had also become a local benefactor through his gift of a thousand acres of land and half a million dollars to build a recreation camp for underprivileged children in his native state.

The speakers at the Prentiss dinner included a senator, an ex-ambassador, a famous scientist, a noted biographer, an Army general, the governor of the state and the president of the university which had just bestowed an honorary degree on Richard Prentiss, once the most obscure of alumni.

All the speakers eulogized the guest of honor, and when the time came for him to respond, an audience somewhat tired of speechmaking wondered how much more oratory it could endure. But Prentiss did not deliver an oration; he spoke simply, colloquially and as if he had quite forgotten that he was now an LL.D.

"We've been listening to some national headliners, men whose names are worth top billing on any program," he began with a shy smile, "and they've been mighty generous about a home-town boy who made good. But I figure they must be surprised that he did . . . and that all of you have a right to be surprised and maybe astounded. So perhaps you'd like to know how it came about. And if anybody here feels cut down to size because he thinks an also-ran like Dick Prentiss has made so good, I'd like to remind him—and maybe this same Dick Prentiss—that there was a time when he'd have had to borrow the price of a pair of tickets for my wife and me to get to this dinner!

"Borrowing used to be part of my act. There are a lot of fellows here tonight who used to stake me when I needed money to buy material for the pots and pans, with which I was forever tinkering, or to send my boys to camp when I didn't have the wherewithal, which was most of the time.

"When we cleared out of here thirty years ago, I was bankrupt and expected to stay that way. I'd lost faith in myself and didn't have any other faith. I'd also lost my job at the bank, because I did too much homework on my pots and kettles at night to be alert enough to spot a phony twenty-dollar bill in the morning.

"But my wife's family managed to wangle a place for me in a bank in the East, and Alice baked cakes for the women's exchange, and we went on as usual for a few more lean years.

"I woke up to myself one morning in church. Something came over me when I heard the parson reading: 'Vanity of vanities, saith the Preacher, vanity of vanities; all is vanity. What profit hath a man of all his labour which he taketh under the sun?' There's more to it, and anybody who's curious can look it up in the Book of Ecclesiastes in his Bible.

"It came to me there in church that there was no profit to my labor and never had been. Vanity kept me working in a bank where I'd never get ahead. Vanity kept me tinkering at inventions which didn't amount to shucks. Before that service was over, I'd begun to see that vanity is poison ivy in the home plot of a man's thinking.

"By the time that day was over, I'd done a lot of weeding. And I found plenty of false pride that had to be pulled out along with the other stragglers. False pride was what had me working in a bank instead of clerking in a hardware store where I could handle the stuff that interested me.

"Before the week was out, I had a twenty-dollar-a-week job in a small home-appliance shop. Then Alice started making jams and jellies and salad dressing as well as cake for the women's exchange. Stand up and take a bow, Alice. Your salads are still better than any New York chef can toss!

"Well, folks, with a wife like that, a fellow is bound to make good. Before long I was out on the road with a line of pots and kettles. Some sold. Some didn't. So I found out what was in demand, and when I met other fellows in my line we swapped ideas. Then I got a notion we could pool those ideas. That's how Combined Manufacturing Plants got a start.

"Now I'm coming to the pay-off. Dick Prentiss on his own was never worth the little he earned and wasted on the 'vanity and vexation of spirit' of his stubborn determination to be an inventor—and so a somebody—when all the while he was just a promoter and a good salesman in the making. Until I consulted God about my job, I was an underprivileged man who couldn't earn enough to send his boys to a good vacation camp. Maybe that explains why I want to start a camp for underprivileged boys and girls in the city where a lot of you were so helpful to my youngsters.

"But I've got something a whole lot bigger to pass on than a thousand acres or the money to put a few buildings on the land. I want all of you to share the biggest thing in my life: the knowledge that a man can go into partnership with God when he's willing to put aside his vanity and pride and let God be the senior partner in all his enterprises.

"So now, if any of you fellows think Dick Prentiss has turned out to be a credit to the home town, don't forget to 'give God the glory' for what mind, the senior partner, showed me how to do."

"Except the Lord build the house, they labour in vain that build it. . . ." (Psalm 127:1, the Psalm which David wrote for his son Solomon.)

If you have never been able to find your right place in the world, if you feel like a misfit, and if you feel that you have come to the end of your road, why not try another road? All you need do is turn unreservedly to God and ask for guidance. Pray for vision so you may recognize God under the name and in the manifestation which comes to you, because it best expresses the nature of the Supreme Being to your thought.

Wisdom has always been available to those who searched for it with all their hearts and with confident, open, receptive minds. Some are inspired through recognizing that "Love never faileth." Some are uplifted when they learn that "It is the spirit that quickeneth" man's perception. But the working of God's law will come to each in the manner in which he is best qualified to receive it.

> And thine ears shall hear a word behind thee, saying, This is the way, walk ye in it, when ye turn to the right hand, and when ye turn to the left.

The awareness of inherent ability, the inspiration for right activity, the assurance of what the individual is best equipped to do lie dormant in his own consciousness. When success along beaten paths has eluded a man, as it eluded Richard Prentiss for many years, what he most needs is a humble willingness to let himself be guided. Humility enables a man to hear the voice of inspiration when it speaks, but that voice and its message cannot come to any man until he has quieted the clamor of his own thoughts and prepared to listen to the instruction of spirit.

Always and under all conditions man has to become aware of his gifts before he can develop them and put them to use. Honest self-evaluation is not easy for the vain or the arrogant, but every man's potentials must be brought to the light of conscious awareness and evaluated in that light before they can be of any use to him.

Our pioneer ancestors had to read by candlelight, because they had no idea that there was a more satisfactory way of illuminating their houses. But even if nobody had any knowledge of it, all the elements (the potential) for hundred-watt bulbs existed long before Benjamin Franklin's kite suggested the relation of lightning and static electricity. In order to think his way to a more luxuriously equipped future man had to extend the frontiers of his inventiveness beyond kerosene lamps and natural-gas burners and Welsbach mantles. But when men assemble ideas, set the limitless power of intelligence to work, and ally themselves and their efforts with that intelligence they go forward beyond the tight little frontiers of the moment in which they are living.

You and I can learn to drive our cars without knowing anything of the principle of thermodynamics. We can live out our days without knowing anything of the principle of being. But would you trust yourself to a car whose engine was built by men who had not studied the laws having to do with the conversion of heat into mechanical energy? Then is there any wisdom in trusting yourself to beliefs and theories which have no basis in, nor knowledge of, the workings of intelligence?

The Psalmist wrote: "Be still, and know that I am God. . . ." It is always possible and never too late to learn to be still, quiet and receptive to the ideas through which creative intelligence reveals itself to human consciousness. There is no other security so great as the mental security which grows out of a lively awareness that man has a heaven-bestowed ability to think logically and to put the consequent inspirations into operation. There is no satisfaction so complete as that which derives from expecting God to be on your side, because you are seeking to learn which is His side and to take it when it is revealed to you.

This is the way to go into partnership with God. It is a partnership that will never fail, and it cannot be dissolved unless you willfully choose to turn away from what "forever seeks to bless." For mind, invoked and implemented through its human agency, man, will never mistake the right direction, go on strike, or cease to operate in your behalf.

9

A CANDLE OF UNDERSTANDING

I shall light a candle of understanding in thine heart, which shall not be put out.

—THE APOCRYPHA, II ESDRAS 14:25

A HUMOROUS philosopher of the past decade used to tell the story of Tomas, a blustering Spanish peasant, whose harsh voice was forever nagging at his wife and cursing his luck, which he did nothing to improve. Of all the vineyards on the slopes beyond Malaga those of Tomas yielded the poorest grapes. Stones and weeds choked his land. It had too much shade and too little drainage, and Tomas found it more congenial to complain, because his grandfather had chosen the least desirable land in the province, than to dig out the stones. It was not until his oldest son, Pedro, was eight and big enough for heavy work that there were ditches in the hillside.

Finally a year came when Tomas' grapes were bigger and juicier than those of his neighbors, and he got an excellent price for the vintage. He did not thank the dear

God for sending rain and sun in due proportions. He did not thank his wife, Ana, for pruning the vines. He did not thank Pedro for irrigating the slope. He did not offer them a single one of the gold pieces his grapes had brought. He stuffed the money in his saddlebags, put on his holiday clothes and ordered Pedro to saddle the mule. When all was accomplished he leaped upon the beast and announced that he was going to Madrid.

"God willing," Ana said piously.

"I am going to Madrid!" Tomas repeated and kicked the poor mule.

"But the beast is old, and it will be a hard journey for him over the mountains," Ana said. "It will take a long time to go and come again, and how shall our children eat while you and the mule are away?"

"A little extra labor will not hurt you and Pedro," Tomas growled. "A little rest will not hurt me. A man whose vineyards were once the worst in his village and are now the best has earned the right to see something of the big world. I am going to Madrid!"

"God willing," Ana sighed.

Tomas swelled out his chest, puffed out his cheeks and popped his eyes with rage. "Out of my way, woman," he shouted. "I am going to Madrid! You shall not stop me! Not you and not your God!"

Ana could not be certain he had really spoken the blasphemous words.

Now she saw a big bullfrog in the saddle where Tomas had been, and after a moment the creature leaped down and hopped off toward the pond where the ducks swam. Ana ran to the water, and there was the largest frog she had ever seen, splashing around and croaking the hoarsest "brek-kek-koek" she had ever heard.

"Oh, Tomas!" she called. "If that big warty frog is indeed you, pray to God and ask him to forgive you, and I am certain he will change you back to a man again."

She got no answer save an angry croaking from the other side of the pond; so she unsaddled the mule, took a gold piece from the saddlebags, told Pedro to look after his brothers and sisters, and hurried to the village to buy a candle for St. Tomas.

When she got home from the shrine, where she had lighted her candle and said her prayers, she went at once to the pond and called her husband's name. As she stood on the bank a big bullfrog hopped out of the water, and in another second there was Tomas, shaking his fist at her and croaking in his harshest voice.

"Stop trying to interfere with my plans!" he shouted. "Enough time has been wasted. Find Pedro at once and tell him to saddle the mule."

So Ana ran to do as her man had ordered, and as she went she stumbled and wept because Tomas had neither embraced her nor thanked her for the prayers and the candle which had made him a man again. She fetched Pedro and the mule back from the fields they had been turning, and at once Tomas flung the saddlebags over the beast, leaped up on its back and kicked his heels against its thin flanks.

"Where are you going?" Ana asked.

"To Madrid!" Tomas boomed.

"God willing," she replied.

"To Madrid or back to the frog pond!"

Tomas' harsh voice broke; and while Ana and Pedro stood watching, the mule began kicking up its heels for joy because the heavy saddle was empty. Then a big bullfrog at the edge of the pond started croaking so furiously that it sounded like cursing.

"To Madrid or back to the frog pond" is the leitmotiv of many unfinished symphonies.

Anyone given to swelling out his chest and talking of his determination to express himself and live his life in his own way had better make sure that he is not another Tomas.

There cannot be a satisfying outcome for anyone who stubbornly persists in a way of life and on a pattern of achievement for which he is not equipped and for which everyone around him will have to pay.

> The common problem, yours, mine, every one's
> Is—not to fancy what were fair in life
> Provided it could be,—but, finding first
> What may be, then how to make it fair
> Up to our means.

In those lines of Robert Browning's there is no hint of fatality or weak submission to whatever comes along. The poet is saying that our problem is to evaluate our ability in terms of what it is logical to believe an honest, intelligently directed effort can make of it. He counsels supporting our efforts with faith and understanding and evaluating our dreams before we try to make them come true.

Some years ago a well-known musician opened a vocal studio in a small New England town. Among the first to enroll was a choir singer from a city twenty miles away. The young man subscribed to three lessons a week, and he never missed one of them. He and his little jalopy appeared at the studio three times a week regardless of snow or sleet or rain.

As the weeks passed it became increasingly evident that the young man had no "fire," no dramatic understanding, no power of interpretation, no equipment, but a pleasant little voice and a large determination to make it serve his purpose to become "another Caruso." The tenor was neither an artist nor a musician. The teacher was both, and a man of integrity as well; so one day he asked the student if he had ever considered any career other than singing. Then the tenor said that he had been within a year of his degree as an electrical engineer when he decided that he wanted to make singing his profession. He added that he had been at the top of his class in engineering and that his professors had been very enthusiastic about his future.

"*Had* been?" the vocal teacher said. "Aren't they enthusiastic now?"

The pupil said he had given up his college work in order to devote himself to his art. He explained that the money his father, a cobbler, could spare for his son's education was not sufficient to pay for courses in both engineering and singing and that he preferred his art to science.

Then the teacher decided that it was time for the tenor to face the truth.

"But you have no 'art,'" the teacher explained. "You have nothing but a pleasant little voice. That is not enough for a successful career. To be a great singer takes even more than a great voice. It requires temperament, musicianship, 'fire,' dramatic ability, feeling, fervor and the magic of genius. You sing 'I adore you, my beloved' and 'Please pass the bread' with equal fervor—or lack of it. Now you tell me that your professors at college say you will be a successful engineer.

"I am compelled by honesty and experience to tell you that you will never be a successful singer. There is no hope for you to become a star. You are not a soloist but a choir singer. Don't waste your time or your father's hard-earned money. Don't disappoint the good man who has already given you three years of college. Go back and work for your degree. Develop a profession that will support you. If you do that, you can afford to sing for your own enjoyment. But the public will never pay to listen to your voice. So I'd be a crook to take your money for lessons that can never give you what you lack."

The singer turned on the teacher angrily and said, "If you don't want my thirty dollars a week, I'll find someone who does!"

It was not hard for the stubborn young fellow to find someone to give him singing lessons; but no one could give him the gift of song. So, after five years of wasted effort this young Tomas is still a frog croaking in a pond.

The ability to evaluate one's desires and one's talents, to seek attainable goals and to work toward them under the guidance of wisdom rather than of willfulness is a gift almost as great as genius itself. There is a vast difference between determination and stubbornness. Determination measures and studies boundaries and the limitations they fix; it strengthens resolve and the willingness to work for accomplishment in a field where it is reasonable to expect results. Stubbornness is tough and unyielding; it works in the dark and without legitimate reason to expect success.

The arrogant and self-centered are not patient enough, farsighted enough or humble enough to make an intelligent evaluation of themselves and their abilities. Perhaps the chief reason why the meek are blessed is because they are willing to take their hopes and their dreams to God in prayer; and it is not the arrogant but the meek who have been promised that they shall inherit the earth.

Achievement rests on a firmer foundation than mere desire. If you are one of those with an overweening desire to set out for some Madrid of your choosing, make sure before you start that your going does not work great injustice on those you leave behind you, that you know the road to your goal and that you have a design for living in Madrid after you reach it.

Before the wise man starts on a journey or dedicates

himself to a project, he meditates or prays for guidance. He opens his thought to inspiration and illumination. He lights a candle of understanding in his heart to show him the way.

The blindness of self-will cannot persist in the philosophy of a man who has lighted his "candle of understanding." He will discern the path he should take, perceive the distant goal through the uncertain mists of the "Tomas-thought" and go forward with new confidence along the road of wisdom.

Real, lasting and satisfying success comes to those who are willing to seek for guidance and follow it when it appears, to those who are satisfied to channel their abilities into the form of activity for which they are best suited.

Genius has been called "an infinite capacity for taking pains," for working to develop talent to complete expression. But first, and let us not forget this even for a minute, it is wise to take the measure of the talent. We are free to choose our goals, but unless we use that freedom wisely and in the light of understanding it can turn us away from the heights we are equipped to reach and send us off on a detour leading nowhere.

When you and I discipline ourselves and moderate our desire for self-expression (without knowing precisely what our true selfhood is), you and I can arrive at harmony and understanding. Each of us must also recognize that the other fellow has a desire to express himself and his theories, and one has no more right than the other to enforce his will. Any other attitude is a bland denial of the very thesis of our Declaration of Independence. Not only are all men created free and equal, but each man is created in the image and likeness of God. Why not let God express Himself? Why not train ourselves to beware of the "many inventions" of a series of human opinions emanating from a crowd of independent operators—each intent on his own way—and learn to say and mean and think in terms of "Thy will be done"?

Twenty years ago a certain college town was scandalized by the goings on in one of its most prominent families. Ralph, the youngest son of Dr. Maxon of Maxon College, flunked out of high school in his senior year. The boy came from a family of intellectuals. One of them had been a founder of the college; and in every generation, in the long years since, there had been a Maxon as president or chairman of the board or—at the very least—as a department head. It was unthinkable and disgraceful that a son of this tradition should have low grades all through high school and fail miserably in his final exams. The town buzzed with the shame Ralph had brought on his family, and Dr. Maxon took time out from the affairs of the college to deal with the culprit on the home front.

Ralph proudly—or stubbornly, as Dr. Maxon thought—called his father's attention to his A's in drawing and botany and said he could have had a couple of A pluses in the things he liked if he hadn't had to waste so much time in stuff like math and physics, which were tough for a fellow who didn't enjoy them. He begged his father to send him to an Eastern art school, and even as far east as Paris if it didn't cost too much. Dr. Maxon announced that he did not intend to have a Bohemian, a crazy painter, in his family. No son of his was going to become an artist or go to an Eastern school. If Ralph did not want to be a professor, he could study law or banking or business administration which, like teaching, had dignity and importance. Maxon College was the place for a Maxon. Ralph would have to be tutored all through the summer, and if he did well, he might be able to pass his entrance examinations without going back and taking his senior year in high school over again. This, said Dr. Maxon, was his final word on the subject.

That evening Ralph Maxon was arrested for drunken driving. His car had run up onto the sidewalk and had smashed a plate-glass window in the most important store on Main Street.

Dr. Maxon refused to furnish bail for his scapegrace son or to permit anyone else to furnish it. He said a few days behind bars might have a salutary effect on young Ralph, who quite obviously would have to learn the hard way.

In the morning it was found that Ralph had broken out of jail. Twenty-four hours later he was still missing. Dr. Maxon paid the fines and hired a detective agency to trace the prodigal son. But nothing was heard from or of young Ralph.

After five years everyone considered him decently dead and the family, excepting the boy's mother, were somewhat relieved. Then one midsummer day an eminent clergyman from the Far West came to call at President Maxon's house, and the problem of the prodigal son took a new turn.

"A man of mystery has been working on my land as a gardener for the better part of a year," the white-haired visitor announced. "I've just found out who he *was* and why he prefers being who he *is*. I've traveled more than a thousand miles to tell you the story of our Max, who turns out to be your Ralph. He didn't think you'd be interested in what I have to tell you about him. I do. Am I right, sir?"

Dr. Maxon said his visitor was right, and asked if the story was such that Mrs. Maxon could hear it without being hurt. The clergyman smiled and said he thought the account was one Mrs. Maxon should not miss.

"Last summer," said the clergyman, "a hungry 'stumblebum,' as he called himself then, came to our place and asked for a handout. Our gardener had left because of illness and the whole place showed signs of neglect. I asked the tramp if he would be willing to earn his meal and said he could have a night's lodging to boot if he'd cut the grass. There's an acre of it around the house and a couple of slopes out to the orchard that had grown high and wide and not too handsome since our gardener started going to seed. The boy cut all the grass, watered it and for full measure he pruned the roses and weeded my wife's cutting garden. He looked all in and half starved when he was through, but he asked if he could wash before he ate.

"God gave my wife the vision to discern the real man behind the beard and the bitterness on that young face, and she said, 'Son, wouldn't you like to shave too before you come to supper with us?'

"I don't know whether it was the way he kissed her hand for this or the way he handled his knife and fork that I needed to convince me, but next morning I was ready to ask him if he'd like to stay on and make something of our garden. He stayed. He disappeared once for two days and came back smelling of liquor and looking mighty seedy again, but he came back.

"Then my wife started plying him with milk and asking him to drive her around in her little roadster. Naturally he had to have a decent suit for that, and I told him to go off and get him an outfit and charge it to me. He didn't take advantage of that, either. My wife and I were calling him 'son' by that time, and feeling kind of proud of him.

"The first time he drove my wife to my church he didn't come in. When I asked him if he thought I was an old fogey and my sermon would bore him, he muttered something about not wanting to neglect the delphinium. But after that he came to church every Sunday morning.

"Well, folks, our garden is a show place now, but neither one of us is as proud of it as we are of the boy.

"A week ago I told him I'd never met a greater artist with growing things, and I said he actually painted with flowers and that I'd like to stake him to a course at our state agricultural college: landscape gardening or any form of floriculture or horticulture he was of a mind to study. That's when he broke down and told me the story of a youngster who thought he was all through at eighteen.

"So I'm here to tell you that we'll be proud to take your boy into our home as our own son if it's all right with you. He doesn't think it will matter to you one way or the other. He's not bitter about it; he just says you can't be expected to care. But I, being a preacher, would like to deliver a short sermon if it's all right with you."

The Maxons agreed that it was, and the white-haired visitor went on. "The boy is made in the image and likeness of God, not in yours or your great grandfather's, Dr. Maxon. He's come to see that he was as stubbornly set on being his own man five years ago as you were on having him your man. *But he's God's man.* And this particular, individual son of our Father is a fine gentleman but no scholar. He's himself, but that self is an artist, not a college professor. Because I see this, he's more my son than yours, Dr. Maxon. If you subcribe to this, my wife would like the two of you to come out and spend a month with us and our son on our place this summer. It's a beautiful garden spot, because a wonderful young artist with flowers has made it that way."

Today Ralph is one of the foremost floriculturists in his part of the country. When he landscapes a place he paints with flowers and shrubs and trees, and the Maxons are proud of him. They spend three months of every year in the fairyland where Ralph lives with the good samaritans who trusted their souls' invincible surmise, took a "stumblebum" into their home and helped him find himself.

A quatrain by Thomas Hardy expresses the thing that all set, stubborn, self-willed and basically insecure natures must recognize before they can come to terms with life.

> Let me enjoy the earth no less
> Because the all-enacting Might
> That fashioned forth its loveliness
> Had other aims than my delight.

10

LADDER TO THE SKIES

A picture is not wrought
By hands alone, good Padre, but by thought.
In the interior life it first must start,
And grow to form and colour in the soul;
There once conceived and rounded to a whole,
The rest is but the handicraft of art.

—William Wetmore Story,
"Padre Bandelli Proses"

In the days when automobiles were dubbed horseless carriages and viewed with skepticism, Roy Wayne became aware that he was living in an inventive age and began trying to dream up some contrivance that would make his name and his family's fortune. He was a successful traveling salesman, and he prided himself on being a keen observer. Before long he recognized what a tedious process it was to label bottles by hand and hit on the notion of constructing a machine to take over the job. He figured it out, found someone to draw a blueprint under his direction, sold the idea of building the thing to an expert machinist, and then used his supersalesman tactics to persuade a wealthy acquaintance to back his project.

It was all of six months before the labeling machine started to function. But finally the bottles went sliding over the conveyer belt at measured intervals and without piling up into a log jam; the sponge and the feeder were coming down at the exact moment when there was a bottle beneath them waiting to be moistened and topped with a label; and the bottles were again on hand when the plunger came down to affix the labels.

The machinist, draftsman and backer sighed with relief. At last they had a labeling machine! Then Roy Wayne became conscious of a detail which had hitherto escaped him: the bottlers of soft drinks, his potential customers, labeled their containers on both neck and body. That meant a second set of labels and plungers and feeders of a much smaller arc than those already installed; so it was evident to Roy that his machine would have to be retooled before he could market it.

The machinist cursed but went to work on the problem; the backer growled but went out to raise more funds; but Roy Wayne began getting bored by his labeling machine and the difficulties which hindered its completion. He started hatching a project for packaging dry groceries and looking for people to develop his idea and finance it.

Anyone who has ever watched cardboard boxes rhumba down the assembly line in a gay little dance and arrive at the end of the conveyer belt filled with cereal or soap flakes will know what an idea Roy had dreamed up this time. But again the problems arose, and the difficulties appeared, and he was irked by the delays and began to cast around for another idea.

He got it. This time it was a plan for obviating the medicine-dropper approach to fountain pens and building them with inner tubes. He was convinced that this self-filling apparatus would be a big thing, and he was determined to be first in the rich field. He persuaded his backer to rush into an advertising campaign and to take a quarter page in a national weekly of wide circulation. Before production on the Wayne pen was advanced to the stage where it could take care of the orders, they began coming in from dealers all over the country.

Long before Wayne Associates was ready to make delivery on the prematurely promoted pen, a far superior one was on the market. Once again, when the thread of his imagination got snarled with the practical details of actual production, Roy Wayne lost interest in the work at hand and sent his fancy galloping off in a new direction.

He never thought an idea through to a successful conclusion. He never stayed with a concept until it became a product. When he died at eighty Roy Wayne was still planning his great achievement. Of a dozen devices which he first imagined and then abandoned, at least half are now commonplaces of daily living.

Heaven is not reached at a single bound;
  But we build the ladder by which we rise
  From the lowly earth to the vaulted skies,
And we mount to its summit round by round.

But most of us want to skip a round or two! We know the fable of the hare and the tortoise, but how many of us apply it to ourselves?

The world is well stocked with Roy Waynes. Their very richness of imagination may defeat them. They go running up the ladder of accomplishment so fast they run themselves out of breath. They don't concentrate or contemplate. They don't know that *self*-confidence is not enough for real achievement. It takes confidence in the idea itself and in the source of the idea to keep a man faithful to his dream and willing to labor to make it come true.

Inspired thought is on a different level from that of everyday taken-for-granted thinking. It demands respect, honesty, loyalty and faithful development.

Success comes to those who stay with their ideas, who think them through and work them out. Like the emotional philanderer, the mental philanderer doesn't know the real thing when he finds it.

If you are what the world calls an inventive genius and have never reaped a reward from any of the original ideas which have come to you, isn't it about time for you to examine your situation from a new angle?

Failure is not a matter of luck or chance. It stems from faulty planning. There should be four cardinal points in your blueprint for success, and here they are:

1. *Organize your concepts before you make projects of them.* Don't go all out to build a "labeling machine" until you know just what will be expected of it.

2. *Evaluate your will to work—steadily, faithfully, patiently—until you have built your idea into a completed whole.* Don't let difficulties bore or discourage you, but see them as challenges, as incentives, to more and better work on your part.

3. *Support your physical and mental efforts with spiritual steadfastness.* Don't forget that ideas come from mind, the source of intelligence, and that it is natural for the ideas of mind to be fulfilled.

4. *Cultivate humility and confidence in good.* Don't forget that "it is God which worketh in you both to will and to do of his good pleasure." This is the crux of the whole matter, for the humble man is open-minded. He keeps his thought alert, receptive to new ideas. He is not stubborn or opinionated. He is willing to edit his plans whenever he gets more light and sees the wisdom of changing his original conception. Don't forget that perspective enhances perception.

Down through the years there have always been pioneers in advance of their times. Not only did they have to sharpen their inventiveness in order to develop their ideas, but they had to find courage with which to face the unbelief of the skeptic, the suspicion of the conservative and the danger of betrayal by their own doubts and uncertainties. They had to perceive the value of their ideas and to dedicate themselves to the work required to develop those ideas. As George Eliot wrote:

Antonio Stradivari has an eye
That winces at false work and loves the true.

Stradivarius was loyal to his magnificent genius. It is told that he would not permit his name to be signed to the violins he made in the later years of his life, because he was afraid that his fading eyesight might have permitted some slight flaw in his work to pass unnoticed.

The man who builds a violin, like the man who builds a machine, produces a masterpiece when, and only when, he is faithful to his highest ideal and willing to work to bring it to completion.

In 1831 a poor farm boy born in a log cabin in the West Virginia back country rattled out of his father's barnyard on a reaper he had invented and constructed. Cyrus McCormick lived forty miles from a blacksmith shop and even farther from a railroad or canal. In order to build his machine he had been compelled to dig ore out of the Alleghenies and smelt it himself in a furnace of his own contriving.

For ten years he tried in vain to sell one of his harvesters, and in the next five years he managed to find buyers for less than a hundred of them. But he persisted. At the time of the Civil War there were some fifty thousand harvesters in the fields, and the machine released thousands of men for duty at the front. Today there are American harvesting machines in every part of the world where grain is grown. It is grown on thousands of acres of land which it would have been impractical to cultivate if the farm boy's reaper—and the machines of which it was the forerunner—had not been available to harvest the vast crops.

A flash of inspiration is not enough to lead to the invention of a harvester or the laying of the Atlantic cable. It takes perseverance to crystallize concept into idea, and idea into construction and the will to work, and thus work out the wonders no man can accomplish unless he is "loyal to the royal" in himself, faithful to the vision which creative intelligence itself has given him.

When the "voice of God" spoke to men in Biblical times, they received the messages because they were listening for them and were willing to revalue their human theories and opinions and ambitions in the light of inspiration. But before any one of the world's great leaders could show others the way to liberation, he had to free himself from doubt and fear. The Book of Joshua states this effectively; it shows how the receptive thought is lifted out of the darkness of self-detraction and into the light of confidence in God.

Before Moses died in the land of Moab, he delegated Joshua to carry on his work; but Joshua doubted himself and doubted also that the people would follow him if he were to attempt to lead them. So he prayed and listened humbly for the word which should guide him, and his receptive thought opened to receive the message set down in the first chapter of the book which bears his name: " . . . as I was with Moses, so I will be with thee: I will not fail thee, nor forsake thee. . . . Be strong and of a good courage; be not afraid, neither be thou dismayed: for the Lord thy God is with thee whithersoever thou goest."

"Be strong and of a good courage" came to his thought three times, and then he received the command to observe all the law and meditate upon it, "for then thou shalt make thy way prosperous, and then thou shalt have good success."

These rules apply to our times. Broaden your vision to include God, and you will find confidence with which to meet the challenge of today. Become aware that God governs, and you will gain the serenity required for completing your work. If you are tired and bewildered and discouraged, if you are struggling in the dark of confusion and conjecture and uncertainty and cannot see light ahead, try looking up, rather than down, or ahead! Read Psalm 91, or 23, or 139, or all of them. Ponder them. Stay with them until their beauty and their promise are incorporated into your thinking; for when men turn earnestly to God for help and counsel, when they pray for His directing, spiritual insight gives them the assurance which the Psalmist expressed in these lovely phrases:

> Thy word is a lamp unto my feet, and a light unto my path. (Psalm 119:105)

Those who are conscious of the somethingness of mind know that it blots out the stultifying belief that the nothingness of ignorance can interfere with, block or defeat the potency of intelligence in action. Knowing always destroys not knowing!

Any man can drive out the bogey of discouragement, the goblin of defeat, by positive absolute knowing that he is able to govern his own thinking. The big job which none can escape is to claim and practice dominion over thought. When that has been done man finds himself at the point of achievement natural to the perceptive who are also receptive and responsive to the guidance which Joshua sought as Moses before him had done.

Of course, there are individuals who refuse to be guided and who act as if preserving their own individuality would be endangered by letting the light of wisdom and inspiration into their consciousness. They say, "I've got to work this out my own way. I've got to be myself or I'm nothing."

Marilyn Carter was one of those people who are stubbornly determined to be themselves even if they don't know much about their selfhood. She was given to quoting a bit of George Borrow's *Lavengro* to anyone who ventured to suggest that it might be wise to modify her concept of M. Carter a bit: "O ye gifted ones, follow your calling, for however various your talents may be, ye can have but one calling capable of leading ye to eminence and renown; follow resolutely the one straight path before you . . . let neither obstacles nor temptations induce ye to leave it. . . . Turn into other paths, and for a momentary advantage or gratification, ye have sold your inheritance, your immortality."

Those lines fortified and justified Marilyn's determination to immortalize herself as a pianist. She loved beauty; she wanted to put more of beauty into the world. She would not listen when a critic of standing assured her that pianists of her caliber were a dime a dozen and that most of them couldn't get even half a dozen engagements during a twelve-month year. Marilyn declined to deviate from the path she had chosen; she persuaded her father to give her a musical education and a concert grand piano and to finance a recital at the opening of each winter season. But nothing came of it—not even good notices.

When Marilyn was in her early thirties and still unknown in the world of music, her father died, and she fell heir to an estate consisting chiefly of debts.

The lawyer who had been appointed administrator salvaged a few hundred dollars for Marilyn and advised her to spend it on a course at a good business college and train her facile fingers to operate a typewriter instead of a piano. He assured her that it would pay better, and to prove it he offered her a position at a living wage if she would prepare herself for work in his office. So Marilyn moved herself and her concert grand piano into a one-room studio and spent most of her little legacy on a course at a secretarial school. In time she went to work for her legal adviser at what she regarded as a stopgap job by which to finance her weekly piano lessons.

During the first year of her business career, Marilyn worked for her father's friend and was paid much more than she was worth. All that prosperous year she chattered to her fellow workers about the career which she was going on with as soon as she had saved enough to hire a good publicity representative and a hall. In time she talked herself out of her position and of several subsequent and not so well paid jobs.

Eventually she got work as a receptionist in the studio of Lora Amesbury, a well-known interior decorator. The salary was generous, the duties were assorted. Sometimes Mrs. Amesbury asked her receptionist to match samples of velvet or brocade during her lunch hours. Sometimes she requested Miss Carter to stop on her way home and deliver a bit of china or glass to a client whose place she was going to pass en route. Marilyn never protested; she remembered the lean years and did not risk telling Mrs. Amesbury that she was not an errand girl. That might lead to her having to become one.

Before long she began finding her overtime work delightful. The Amesbury clients did not treat her as if she were an errand girl; they asked her to stay and have a cup of tea and plied her with little cakes and questions about flower arrangements and furniture groupings. Marilyn liked visiting in luxurious surroundings; she enjoyed being consulted on matters of *décor;* she reveled in opportunities to indicate that she was marking time in the Amesbury Studio while developing her own career as a pianist.

One day she was summoned into the dramatic chartreuse and orchid and turquoise office which made such a perfect setting for the vivid Mrs. Amesbury. Marilyn's employer was curt and businesslike as she told her brusquely that if she wished to go on working in the studio, she would have to stop boring its patrons with autobiographical details.

"My clients are drawn to you," Mrs. Amesbury said, "because you are so distinguished-looking and have such a way with flowers. They are repelled by your chatter about being a frustrated prima donna of the pianoforte. I'd be sorry to lose you, but much sorrier to lose one of my clients because of your condescension to a profession not unrelated to the arts. Whether you stay here or not is up to you, Miss Carter. Shall we wait a fortnight for you to adjust to the facts?"

Long before the fortnight was over, Marilyn had made her adjustment. She liked her work. She admired Mrs. Amesbury. She did not feel condescending or patronizing about the art of decorating. She recalled a line of Christopher Marlowe's: "What is beauty; saith my sufferings, then . . . "

She asked herself, "Well, Carter, what *is* beauty? Can't you find it in anything but music? There's magical beauty in the colors I have a flair for matching, in the draperies I like to help design, in the flower arrangements for which I appear to have a very real gift. Why, I'm having a wonderful career, and I hope I haven't done myself out of it just when I'm starting to succeed at it."

At this point Marilyn cried a little over her lost dreams of another kind of success. She felt exceedingly sorry for a pathetic Marilyn Carter who would never hear the world applauding her beautiful piano playing.

Then, almost as brusquely as Mrs. Amesbury might have spoken, she admonished herself: "But you've found a way of pleasing your public, a beautiful and rewarding way. You help to bring out beauty in people's homes and so in their lives. You couldn't do a better thing if you were Dame Myra Hess! And nobody has ever told you that decorators like you come a dime a dozen. Make sure they never do say it!"

The next morning she marched humbly into Mrs. Amesbury's office and told her employer something of what was in her heart and that she hoped she might stay on and become a worth-while decorator.

Then Mrs. Amesbury smiled and said, still brusquely, "I need an assistant. From the beginning I've suspected that you have what it takes. Now I know it and so do you! If you are willing, I'll pay for some courses I think you should have, since decorating is a matter of technique as well as of artistic feeling. Maybe the firm will be Amesbury and Carter someday."

And it is. Marilyn still has a concert grand piano in her living room, and she still plays Chopin and Schumann and Debussy without any great distinction. But Mrs. Amesbury gets some of her best inspirations while listening to her partner's music.

Ellen Jones failed as a playwright but became a star copy writer for a big advertising agency. Philip Brown did not make good as a concert violinist, but he became an outstanding concert manager. Arnold Smith could not sell his illustrations, but he can sell insurance. Margo

White did not make a name for herself as an actress, but her tearoom has a very good name and the food to justify it. Each of them had to face the fact that the world will pay for what it likes and that the desire to be a Caruso has to be fortified not only by musicianship but by vocal chords.

A famous milliner acknowledged that she came near breaking her heart and smashing her marriage because she was so set on being an opera singer. But one day an honest teacher said to her, "Forget about warbling, honey. You haven't the tonsils for it. But if it's true that you make your own hats, you have the fingers for that, and I hear millinery pays off better than singing in the chorus, which is the best you can hope for if you insist on making your career with your voice."

No work pays off unless the laborer has good tools and the ability to use them. No profession leads to success unless the artist has the dedication and assurance and serenity which come from the knowledge that "Every good gift and every perfect gift is from above, and cometh down from the Father of lights, with whom is no variableness, neither shadow of turning." (James 1:17.)

II

A HOUSE DIVIDED

Look round the habitable world: how few
Know their own good, or knowing it, pursue.
—DRYDEN, *Juvenal*

ONE OF the theories advanced by modern psychology is that man's mode of expression is controlled and governed by four fundamental wishes: (1) the desire for security, (2) for new experience, (3) for response, and (4) for recognition. If all four of these wishes start operating at once in a single human consciousness, conflict is bound to ensue.

The individual who finds himself impelled to go east and west is likely to go nowhere. Cross-purposes block purpose, and until a man knows why he inclines toward two strongly opposed sets of action, he is likely to be torn between them and the decisions concerning them which he cannot bring himself to make.

The great tenor Battistini never sang in the United States. He had many tempting offers to come to this country, but he refused to accept even the most advantageous of the contracts. As an artist he must have craved the response and recognition of the American audience. The magnificent salary New York managers were ready to offer him must have been very tempting, but the great singer was afraid of seasickness. His desire for security outweighed all his other desires; so after one voyage to Buenos Aires Battistini stayed on his own side of the Atlantic.

Psychiatry has made an effort to reconcile man's conflicting wishes by bringing them out into the open where he can evaluate them and balance them against one another. But nobody can divide himself into neat segments partitioned off from one another by a set of tidy walls.

Our wishes encroach on one another. A well-known actress of a decade ago wrecked her career and eventually her life because she could not reconcile her appetites and her ambitions and could not adjust her fastidious love of beauty to what she called her "awkward truck of a body." She craved the exquisite and the delicate, but she was fond of rich food and overindulged until she became a pendulous mass of fat hanging from fine bones meant for grace and beauty.

The task at which she failed, the common task of all sensitive, delicately balanced people, is to learn to reconcile appetite and desire, yearning and ambition, physical craving and mental ideal. Self-indulgence generally develops the least constructive tendencies in an individual's repertoire of qualities. But the well adjusted have learned to mold their wishes and urges into the balanced form in which one desire will not be forever warring with another, blocking it off from expression, and, therefore, frustrating the tormented individual who is driven in half a dozen directions at once and consequently is jerked back from every attempt at progress.

For each of us the wish of the moment may be based on something as unstable as the whim of the moment. Before anyone yields to an urge at the price of an ideal, he would do well to remind himself that the desire of the eyes may be ignoring the promptings of the heart and the warnings of the mind.

The wish for security is fundamental and normal. But if you are obsessed by the longing to be an aviator, you will have to reconcile your desire to fly and your fondness for a quiet, earth-bound life. Face the fundamental facts about yourself, and you are bound to discover what you most want and how many of your lesser wants you are willing to forego in order to achieve the major desire of your being.

If you and I are so intent on physical security that we feel impelled to live inside a stockade, we won't see much of the world outside; and we must not complain if that world does not break into our chosen quietude to offer us any of its awards. The world's prizes go to those who work for them, not to those who decline to cope with life's problems. If you run away or hide in order to escape competition, exertion and danger, you must be reconciled to the fact that drabness and monotony are likely to take over instead of the challenging activity you chose to avoid.

In view of these simple facts, who will deny that your task and mine is to reconcile ourselves to ourselves? We are not doomed to struggle or strive against what we sometimes call unfair competition or bad luck. We are merely being impelled to evaluate our wishes, to balance them against the effort it takes to attain them and to make them serve our spiritual ideals.

We all know people who are thwarted by their own psychological uncertainties, challenged by their inner conflicts and actually wrecked by their own tendency to ambivalence. But even for the most neurotic of life's shadow-boxers there is a solution of the tendency to go nowhere or to try to go in two directions at once. That solution is indicated in Paul's epistle to the Philippians:

> Be careful for nothing; but in every thing by prayer and supplication with thanksgiving let your requests be made known unto God.
>
> And the peace of God, which passeth all understanding, shall keep your hearts and minds . . .

These verses exhort men not to handicap themselves with morbid fears and anxieties. They advocate liberating thought and examining it in the light of spiritual truth and wisdom.

A few years ago Frank Randolph, a popular account executive in a successful advertising agency, found himself growing so confused and edgy that he could hardly drag himself through his day's work. It became increasingly difficult and finally impossible for him to make the clear and positive decisions he had once tossed off with assurance. He slept badly, ate with less and less zest, made a wreck of his once-happy home life and began to quarrel with everyone with whom he had any dealings. Instead of being his firm's amiable trouble shooter he became one of its troublemakers. After he had been involved in several heated arguments at office conferences, he was persuaded to consult a famous psychiatrist.

Six months of treatment uncovered nothing significant. Analysis brought no revealing clue up from long-suppressed memories. Frank became convinced that he was just "bone-tired," and he was persuaded to take a month's leave of absence and go off for a vacation at a tranquil little lake at the foot of the ancient Taconic Hills. After a tortured fortnight he found that the quiet was as nerve-racking as the turmoil of the city had been. A buzzing bee on the windowpane sounded like the New York subway system invading the place. Acting as his own diagnostician, Frank became convinced that he was on the edge of a total crack-up and that the doctor had sent him away because he didn't know what else to do with a nervous and mental wreck.

As a lad in Sunday school Frank Randolph had been taught to take his problems to God in prayer. Though he felt a bit shamefaced about trying that now, he did not know what else to do. In sheer desperation he began praying for help, and a Bible verse he had long since forgotten came back to his conscious thought:

> For my people have committed two evils; they have forsaken me the fountain of living waters, and hewed them out cisterns, broken cisterns, that can hold no water.

The verse haunted him. He began to wonder what broken cisterns he had dug for himself and how he could find his way to a fountain of living waters. Then, verse after verse in a comforting processional, the words of Bible promises came to him; and one night he slept peacefully with a sense of having turned his problem over to the "big boss." Within a week he found himself equipped with a sense of serenity and a conviction that he could think this thing through to a conclusion.

Before his rest cure came to an end he acknowledged to himself that he knew, and could not pretend that he did not know, exactly what was wrong with Frank Randolph.

He was a house divided against itself. He was not happy in his work, because his firm's policy was not one he could wholeheartedly and honestly underwrite. He had been going along with the organization because he was ambitious and wanted a vice-presidency and the vice-presidential salary. During the past year of growing inner conflict he had been trying to ignore what he did not want to acknowledge. But the higher up he got in his firm and its councils, the more aware he was that its methods were not ethical. He had put himself in a spot where he wasn't getting anything out of his success but a perpetual headache and a guilt complex.

He measured his salary and his satisfaction in spending it against the evasions, equivocations and misrepresentations that went into earning it. Then he went back to New York and handed in his resignation.

He was told to take another month off at the firm's expense. He was offered the vice-presidency toward which he had been heading. Finally he was asked to write his own ticket. When he said he had none to write, because he had decided he would like to go it alone, a storm of protest and disbelief went up. The brass hats of the company felt sure he was planning to walk out with some of their best accounts in his pocket. They heckled him until he was driven to acknowledge that he was quitting because he did not like the kind of thinking that went on around the shop, the kind of business that was being exploited, or the methods used to create a demand for it and for destroying competitors' markets.

When the president of the company called Randolph a fool and a modern Galahad in a tone that hinted he meant Judas, Randolph protested.

"I'm not a Galahad," Randolph said. "I'm not a Benedict Arnold either. But I can't be happy playing it your way, and I've got to be happy to do good work and to feel good. I've discovered that I have some ideals which are the most vital things in my life, and if I ignore them, I'm done for. The whole thing is summed up in a pair of lines from a book some of you may have read: 'Thou shalt worship the Lord thy God, and him only shalt thou serve.' "

Before long the report that Frank Randolph was in a tail spin got around. When he opened a small office and the clients did not come, he had to tighten his spiritual belt and remind himself that he had chosen to give up advantage for principle and that he had done it in full awareness that the situation would take a bit of adjustment.

At the end of a long, hard, six months' pull, Frank Randolph was surprised to have a visit from the advertising manager of a very highly rated company. The visitor looked around the two-room office, which was totally lacking in Aubusson carpets, marble statues and modern French paintings. Then he called Randolph, the head of the unpretentious little organization, a simp for not letting his friends know his plans so they could help him get off on the right foot.

Randolph asked why such a desirable client had finally decided to look up a simp. The man laughed and said it had occurred to him recently that Randolph must be a mighty valuable man or his old firm wouldn't be so darn anxious to tell everyone that he wasn't!

Frank Randolph got his first important account that day and two more before the year was out.

As head of his own firm he works harder than ever before; but he is an adjusted, poised man. He has a sense of well-being, because he is not working under protest from his own nature or against his own sense of ethical values. He has reconciled himself to himself.

There is no conflict more stultifying than that between an individual's sense of honesty and what he cannot avoid recognizing as a dishonest desire for success at any price. There is no eluding the salient truth that unless a man is loyal to his own sense of right he cannot achieve a sense of peace, or wholeness, or security.

What can a man trust if he does not trust himself? When aims and ideals clash there can be no tranquillity in a man's heart. "Every kingdom divided against itself is brought to desolation; and every city or house divided against itself shall not stand...." (Matthew 12:25. See also Daniel 5:18-31.)

A man must be at peace with himself and in tune with his highest sense of good, of that ethical satisfaction which derives from living in accord with his awareness of God, or he cannot achieve a true sense of security, of wholeness.

But how many of us see ourselves whole, "complete in him"? Even so great a philosopher as Thomas Carlyle has declared that "The Fraction of Life can be increased in value, not so much by increasing your numerator as by lessening your denominator."

Great Aunt Matilda was an intellectual woman, prominent among the early educators of our country. But when she thought her house was going to be burned down by the Chicago fire, of the nineteenth century, her thinking disintegrated into fractions of which the common denominator was panic. She was convinced that her house was doomed and was determined to save what she could; so she seized a magnificent celadon vase, which stood in a niche at the top of the front stairway, and tossed the priceless specimen of porcelain out the second-story window. Then she raced to the kitchen, stuffed her gray satin evening dress into her big roasting pan and marched triumphantly out to the street, thinking she had managed to save her most valuable possessions. The fire changed its course before it got to her block, but the lovely sea-green vase was smashed to bits and the satin dress was not improved by its stay in a pan recently occupied by a roast of beef.

Great Aunt Matilda had always been austere and critical, and her family was amused and relieved to discover that she was only human and could fly to pieces when hard pressed. But why should it be thought "human" for people to fly to pieces in the face of danger and the apprehension of greater danger to come?

In a standard dictionary the word *apprehend* is defined in part: (1) to think, believe or suppose; and (2) to be apprehensive, to expect calamity, to fear. But the root meaning of *apprehend* is to lay hold of. And when we lay hold of ideas and think, believe or suppose how they will develop, why should we consider it natural, human or logical to proceed from thinking that it looks like rain to believing there's going to be a cloudburst?

The expectation of calamity is sometimes more devastating than anything the actual calamity could cause. To be apprehensive actually means to lay hold of fear and cling to it. And fear paralyzes thought. If fire or flood or hurricane should hit their community, any number of John Does and Mary Roes will meet the challenge with courage. But if their thought becomes involved with apprehensions of flood or fire, John and Mary are likely to worry themselves into a state of nerves which will unfit them to cope with the dreaded danger if it actually attacks.

It is not easy to integrate thinking into an efficient whole when trepidation is fairly shaking one apart. But, on any level of events, when one has more to handle than a single pair of arms can contain, it is wise to carry celadon vases to safe resting places and to toss silks and satins out of windows. When our thinking is sane, unified and all of a piece, we recognize such simple facts and act on them.

There is a natural soundness and wholeness at the core of our real being, because our thinking derives from the source and the Creator of all being. When we become increasingly aware of ourselves as expressions of this creative mind or intelligence, we find ourselves coming into possession of an inner peace and security and a form of self-reliance such as we have never before known. We recognize that in the very nature of creation we are integers and not fractions, individuals and indivisible, and so we gain the assurance of wholeness, completeness within ourselves, and of unity with our source and Creator. This awareness of God and man in his relation to God is our savior.

The spiritual awareness which makes for mental integrity and clear purpose has always been possible for man. It enabled Moses to lead an enslaved people out of physical bondage and into mental freedom. It gave Jesus the power to prove that the Christ, or understanding of man's unity with God, can lift man out of any experience which threatens to enslave and bury him.

But we of today are still in bondage to our fears. You and I may have done much to resolve our conflicts, to reconcile our warring impulses, but we know plenty of people in whom pride, arrogance, stubbornness and boldness are mingled with such seemingly incompatible qualities as sensitiveness, shyness, timidity and tenderness. We call such folks immature, unbalanced, split personalities, or schizophrenics, according to the degree of their instability and our tolerance. But even for the most bewildered and undirected of them all the denominator of inconsistency can be reduced, the numerator of selectivity increased, and the fraction made a whole.

Self-discipline is a prime requisite for integrating a nature which has been indulging its haphazard impulses at random. It is not easy for the fractional man to slow down, to pull himself together, to see life whole and himself as a responsible part of it. The man whose sense of insecurity is stronger than his awareness of the goodness of God does not find it easy to accept the simple fact that there is enough good in the world to go around. His sense of limitation and of consequent frustration hangs like a curtain of mist between him and the field of thought in which he must learn to operate. Behind that curtain objects are blurred: Everyone looks like a potential enemy; everything appears to be a probable menace or obstacle.

Every veil between man and spiritual truth is a curtain of distortion, disproportion and misrepresentation. Until that veil of mist, fantasy and fear is penetrated by the sunshine of truth, the denominator of chance seems great and man a tiny and negligible fraction of it.

Now let me tell you of two fractional people and how one of them was made whole.

Twelve-year-old Andy Concetti was on his way to a reformatory, when he was paroled to his New England grandparents.

His mother, whose maiden name was Jane Alden, had married her Italian dancing teacher and had divorced him when the boy was two. Both his parents married again and set up new households. Andy did not fit into either pattern and was sent to boarding school before he was six. He was expelled from school after school and was called a problem child even before he was suspected of being an incorrigible one. But when he gave one of his stepbrothers a black eye, stole his savings bank and ran away from home, this series of outrages banished him to the grandparents, who received him without much enthusiasm.

Andy was insolent, untidy and sullen. He did not make friends with the children of the Alden neighborhood but identified himself with a rough gang from another part of town. One day he appropriated two loaves of fresh gingerbread and fed his pals with it. Delia, the maid, reported the loss to Grandmother Alden. She took the boy to task for his thieving ways, and the next day her canary's cage was open and the pet gone. Then Grandmother told Grandfather that maybe the boy belonged in a reform school, and Grandfather decided that the immediate way to handle him was to lock him in his room on a diet of bread and water.

Toward evening Ronald Duncan, the model boy from next door, came to the Aldens with the dead canary wrapped in his best handkerchief. He reported that he had found the poor little bird at the foot of the high fence between the Duncan and the Alden back yards. The sympathetic Ronnie was sent home with a big bunch of Grandfather's best Concord grapes, and Andy got a lecture for making friends with the worst young hoodlums in town when a fine boy like Ronald Duncan lived right next door.

Grandfather was pruning his grapes next day when he heard angry shouting from the back yard. It was Andy's voice, and, although the knotted sheets by which the prisoner had escaped still dangled from his window, Andy was perched on the back fence screaming viciously: "Ronnie Duncan's a dirty wop! Here, tattletale, take this for the bird and this from me and see how you like it, you dirty wop!"

A volley of stones went with the volley of words, and as Grandfather rushed to the fence to drag Andy down, he heard Ronnie moaning from the other side of the barrier: "Ouch! Jeepers, my eye's all bloody. Mama, come quick! Concetti's put my eye out! Come help me, Mama! I can't see!"

Andy was flogged this time and locked in the cellar, which had small barred windows. Then Grandfather drove downtown to fetch Ronnie's father, Judge Duncan, and break the news of Ronnie's injury to him.

By the time the two men reached the Duncan place they found Ronnie on the side porch with a strip of adhesive over one eyebrow, an ice bag on his head, a pitcher of lemonade on the table at his elbow and Grandmother and Mrs. Duncan hovering solicitously over him. He had nothing worse than a jagged cut over one eyebrow and a smug look of importance on his face.

Grandmother Alden began to cry when she saw the judge. She asked what the law did to boys like Andy. First he'd attacked his little stepbrother, then he'd killed her canary, and now he'd gone after poor Ronnie. The judge said he would like to deal with his own son before he dealt with Andy.

"Son, have you any reason to believe that Andy killed his grandmother's pet?" the judge asked.

"Why, n-no, sir." The smug look was gone from Ronnie's somewhat cherubic face.

"Know who did?"

"Well, it could of been our cat."

"Why didn't you tell Mrs. Alden that?"

Ronnie bridled. "I couldn't *know,* and I thought Andy was to blame for letting it out of its cage."

"You don't know what it feels like to be in a cage," the judge said curtly. "One more question, Ronnie. Have you any notion why Andy called you a wop?"

"Sure! He wanted to beat me to it. All our crowd call him Concetti the wop!"

As Grandmother and the two men went across to the Alden house, Judge Duncan said he felt sure Andy had freed the canary because he was sorry for it and not because he wanted to spite his grandmother.

Then the judge went to the cellar door and opened it so Andy could come out.

The boy swaggered up to daylight with sullen truculence. "Going to arrest me?" he asked.

"I'm hoping to let you out of your prison," the judge said.

Andy stared. Then he demanded, "How's Ronnie's eye?"

"What would you do if I said he could never see out of it again?" Judge Duncan asked.

"I'd run away. I'm no good. I bring trouble wherever I go. I'm a hotheaded wop like my dad!"

The judge put his hand on Andy's shoulder and said, "Ronnie's all right. And you are too, Andrew. But it's no fun being a New England Alden with a few Italian frills, is it? You can be proud of your ancestry, though."

Andy ignored the comments on himself. "You mean Ronnie can see all right?" he asked. "I didn't put his eye out? He won't be blind? Oh glory! But is he going to have a bad scar?"

"He's not half so badly scarred as you are, Andrew," the judge said gruffly.

The boy gave a choking cry and ran into the house. They found him lying on the Chippendale sofa, where children with muddy shoes do not belong. He was lying face down and sobbing desperately. No one had ever seen the sullen, insolent lad cry till then, and the judge and Grandfather Alden were embarrassed by it. But Grandmother met the unexpected with unexpected understanding.

"I need you, Andrew," she said. "I'm going to make peach ice cream for supper tonight. I'm not strong enough to turn the freezer—never was—and Delia is busy with her canning."

The boy sniffed and choked. "Yes'm," he managed to say, but he did not stir.

Mrs. Alden got out a clean handkerchief and shoved it into the fist under the tear-stained face. "Come along with Granny, Andrew," she said. "When your mother was your age she always turned the freezer for me, and she always got the dasher. If you're as much like our Jane as you look, you ought to be tickled to pieces at having this chance at the dasher."

Andrew sat up, smiling with bewilderment. "What's the dasher, Granny?" he asked. "I never saw anybody make ice cream."

That was the beginning. It was a long hard road. It is not easy to coax a lonely, bewildered, unwanted, undisciplined youngster out of his shell of bitter defensiveness.

Andy had to find a new approach to a world which had done nothing to show him how to integrate himself, how to make a whole boy out of his warring impulses. He had to become aware of himself as Andrew, the Aldens' grandson, a boy in whom their pride and love were involved. He had to be diverted from his concept of Andy Concetti as a fractional lad torn between the Jane Alden and the Guido Concetti elements which had not blended. The boy was not reconciled to the world until he was reconciled to himself.

Today, at thirty-five, he is well-oriented and successful. He says he began to feel like a real person and not a spinning top when his grandmother said she needed him; and he knew then he would do just about anything to make her go on needing him.

Corinna Glayde has a very different problem in fractions. She is a famous career woman and still handsome at fifty. She has divorced four husbands. Her only daughter does not live with her in her twenty-room house and is not connected with Corinna's business. Corinna lives alone in her big mansion. When she feels desperately alone she fills the place with roistering week-end guests, who are proud to boast that they visit the fabulous Mrs. Glayde, though none of them is her friend. Corinna has no friends. She has no time for sentiment or romance. She has known lovers but not love.

Not long ago the eminent head of the House of Glayde addressed a conference of women's organizations. She told her admiring audience that she was a success because she had never for a moment doubted her ability to conquer the world of business. She added crisply that she had been called on to prove herself when she was very young. She had just turned twenty when her husband walked out on her leaving her with less than twenty-five dollars in her purse and a two-year-old daughter to support. It did not occur to her that she and little Evelyn might have to go hungry. She knew she could find a way to take care of her child and herself.

"I knew I'd never be put out on the street because I couldn't pay my rent," Corinna told her audience. "I was sure I'd find a job and make good at it. I started as a file clerk in the firm of which I am now president. I did not let myself be discouraged by twenty dollars a week and long hours and work which I had to learn as I went along. I improvised. I knew I could get ahead. I never let myself doubt myself. So I am speaking from experience and with authority when I tell you that any intelligent woman can make good and make money if she has to. The main thing is to keep knowing you can do it, and then you can!"

Corinna's business life is full and gratifying; but her personal life is empty and tawdry. There is no love in it, no devotion, none of the warm human values which would make it complete. She does not know her own daughter. The men who once loved her are strangers to her now. Some people call her a symbol of success; but actually she is as much a failure as a success, a fraction of the rounded whole she never troubled to become.

Corinna Glayde made it her business to get along with

the people she met at work. She expected the people in her home to get along with her. She never had time to consider her family's interests or discuss their problems. She said she had to conserve her energy for her work. The career woman was a gracious individual. The home woman was a fractious tyrant.

Corinna Glayde has a glamorous and rewarding business career, but that is all there is to her life. It is only a fraction, and its denominator is Corinna's desperate fear of slipping, of wasting herself on what she calls nonessentials, of letting anything infringe on the position and *réclame* she is forever striving to maintain and build.

So we circle back to the fact that fear divides men and women against themselves, and to the parallel fact that no one need be the dupe of his own fear.

Even when you find yourself facing threatening circumstances with what Elizabeth Barrett Browning called "pulses that beat double" you need not fly to pieces, or burn up with indignation, or collapse from terror. You can handle the worst of your fears confidently because it is yours and, therefore, subservient to you when and as you choose to assert your sovereignty over it.

The man of God's creating is whole, an integer; and when man takes his stand on this spiritual truth he need not admit a fraction of doubt, uncertainty, insecurity or trepidation into his mental process. He is free to claim for himself the wholeness and completeness with which God has endowed his creation. As man REAL-izes that he is "complete in him, which is the head of all principality and power" he can prove that he is an integer, an individual of sound integrity and not a mere fraction of a man.

12

THE MEANS OF SOVEREIGNTY

. . . swear to me
That ye will seek hereafter in yourselves
The means of sovereignty.

—Sir Thomas Noon Talfourd, *Ion*

Every man must learn to live with other people as well as with himself. He must learn to live and let live. There is just one answer to the age-old question: "Am I my brother's keeper?" That answer is: "Yes, you are the keeper of your concept of your brother." After a man has learned to recognize, acknowledge and rejoice in his kinship to his Maker, he must learn also to see his brother in that same light of understanding in which he has become joyfully aware of living and moving and having his being.

Man's dominion, his right to "life, liberty and the pursuit of happiness," does not include dominion over his brother. It postulates for each the individual right of self-government which a free society grants to all intelligent, law-abiding adults. In spite of this, our world is well stocked with good, basically kind, and definitely well-meaning folk who do not seek sovereignty in themselves, and through claiming their dominion over self, but by trying to force their domination on others.

Of all the "little foxes that spoil the vines" none is more insidious than that of a determination to run other people's lives, which masquerades as love and is nothing but despotism. Nobody can make himself big by making somebody else small!

The give and take of human relationship begins on the intimate scale of the home, advances through the larger scope of school, community, town and state, and branches out into national and international relationships. Peace in our times must come through the adjusted sense of human relations so superbly stated by Paul in the thirteenth chapter of his first epistle to the Corinthians.

In the King James Version, verses four, five and six read like this:

> Charity suffereth long, and is kind; charity envieth not; charity vaunteth not itself, is not puffed up,
>
> Doth not behave itself unseemly, seeketh not her own, is not easily provoked, thinketh no evil;
>
> Rejoiceth not in iniquity, but rejoiceth in the truth; . . .

In the Moffatt version of the Bible, we find these simple words:

> Love is very patient, very kind. Love knows no jealousy; love makes no parade, gives itself no airs, is never rude, never selfish, never irritated, *never resentful;* love is never glad when others go wrong; . . .

It is of the love, or charity, which makes no parade, gives itself no airs and is never glad when others go wrong that we need to learn if we want to bring the true sense of love, or charity, into our dealings with our brother.

So-called charity often fails, because it is not motivated by love but is based on *self*-love—and that always makes a big parade and vaunts itself and its generosities. What it is likely to do is to force favors on unwilling recipients who are not benefited by ill-timed gifts they don't want, are humiliated by having to accept, and perhaps can't even use.

To take a bowl of homemade soup to the lonely invalid in the apartment next door is a kindness; but it is an intrusion, and perhaps a cruel and destructive one, to take a similar bowl to the neighbor who is working desperately to finish a blueprint so his architectural plans can be entered in an important competition.

When charity is impelled by love it is intelligent and considerate. It recognizes that a sick man needs food and that a healthy one who is working under pressure can feed on enthusiasm and hope. Restraint is never more vital than when the impulse to be noble and to vaunt one's generosity is likely to pauperize, embarrass and annoy one who asks nothing of his would-be benefactor except to be let alone to do his job.

Last winter a shabbily dressed, dejected-looking man slouched into the office of a well-known philanthropist who had been a classmate at college. The visitor had a flat parcel under his arm and said he'd come to ask for the privilege of hanging a few of his paintings in his old friend's office.

"People will see my stuff if it's hanging here," he said. "Some of your visitors may have not only money but also a yen to pick up a bargain in oils. Those pictures ought to bring a hundred apiece. But I'll take ten if I can get it."

"Help yourself to all the space you need, Chet," the philanthropist said. "But don't you want an advance on the consignment?"

The artist's face lighted up with eagerness; but he shook his head, and then flung it back buoyantly. "Thanks, Bill," he said, "but all I need is a stepladder and a good light."

Bill laughed. "No stepladder. I've got picture hooks. Let's hang our exhibit at eye level and not sky it."

Five minutes later the artist marched out of the office whistling.

He was back within the hour.

"Strange are the workings of Providence," he said. "If I'd cadged the tenner I knew you were ready to give me, I'd have made a beeline for the restaurant in the basement of this building. I hadn't varied my diet of crackers and cheese for several days, and if I'd had the price in my jeans, I'd have treated myself to a beefsteak. As it was I got off at the main floor and went out to the street and bumped into a chap I'd have missed if I'd stayed on the elevator. It seems he's been looking for someone to manage his art gallery, and when he ran into me he decided I was his man. I guess he didn't notice how shabby I am. I was walking like a conqueror and feeling like one, because you had offered to stake me and I'd had the guts to skip it. I've a fifty-dollar-a-week job starting tomorrow and enough in my pocket to live on till my salary starts and some to spare for having my other suit pressed. Thanks for making me feel like a man again, Bill."

"You feel like one because you are one, Chet. Now let's go out to lunch and celebrate your first picture sale. My secretary craves one of your paintings if she can have it for that ten dollars she heard you talk about. It would be a great favor to the kid, Chet."

Chet told me the story, and he ended it this way: "That Bill! He had it figured how it would boost my pride to be doing somebody a favor. And we had *filet mignon* for lunch!"

Kindness like that, flavored with the wisdom and love which make for true charity, are what our whole world needs. Such kindness is a normal human expression of the Master's "Peace on earth, good will to men."

The philanthropist was a banker. He could easily have given his friend a check for a large sum. Perhaps that would have satisfied his own pride and boosted his sense of importance; but it would have pauperized the painter.

It would have robbed him of his dignity, and, as it turned out, it would also have interfered with the timing which gave him his opportunity. But since human vanity did not get into the situation there was nothing to turn Chet aside from the divine beneficence which was ready to bless him.

Anyone who has learned for himself how much of beauty and of wisdom lies in the declaration "I would seek unto God, and unto God would I commit my cause" knows the value of living up to those words. So it is natural for one who has begun to turn to his Father for guidance to permit his brother the same privilege.

Years ago when I was a girl reporter and Dorothy Dix was the great lady of newspaperdom, she told me this same thing in her own crisp and twinkling way. A group of us had been invited to the chambers of a famous judge to hear a debate on the wisdom of uniform divorce laws for all the states of the Union. When we were leaving, the reporter from the morning paper of our organization asked me to write her story for her, since she had a big date and wanted an hour's rest before she started off for the evening.

I was ready to agree when Dorothy Dix said firmly, "No, indeed! You can't write Di's story for her. Your style's nothing like hers. You'd both get into trouble. You don't need a beauty sleep, Diana. You're handsome enough without one and not old enough to need one."

Diana tossed her head, hailed a taxi and whirled off to do her own work.

Dorothy Dix and I took the subway, and while we were riding uptown she said, "Listen, child! Your heart is kind. Teach your head how to be kind. It's never a real favor to anyone to let her take advantage of you. It just encourages her to lean till she gets lopsided."

Then she gave me a few more brisk admonitions about the difference between kindness and showy generosity.

"Don't you ever send American Beauties to an old lady who longs for the wood violets she's not spry enough to go out and pick for herself," she said. "And don't you ever get so sorry for anyone that you'll make her so sorry for herself she'll dissolve in tears over her troubles. That never helps. The only way to give unhappy folks a boost is to show them the way to climb out of the Slough of Despond they're mired down in."

Dorothy Dix was a good-humored, wise and helpful oracle because she was constructively kind and not sentimentally gushing. She learned her practical wisdom in the school of hard experience, which nothing in her luxurious youth had indicated she'd ever have to enter. She was born Elizabeth Meriwether, and when she was presented to society she was a pampered Southern belle. In her room she was accustomed to stepping out of her clothes in the middle of the floor and leaving them for one of the servants to pick up. When she became Mrs. Gilmer she stepped into romance.

After a brief period of happiness her husband became a wheel-chair invalid. The progressive malady made him bitter and helpless; so she took over. She had to earn money, and the most promising opportunity that came her way made her what she called a job as a "three-dollar-a-week copy girl and printer's devil." But it was not long before "Dorothy Dix" emerged (like the fabled phoenix!) from the ashes of Elizabeth Meriwether Gilmer's lost dreams.

Long after she reached the years when most old ladies would have felt justified in sinking back into preoccupation with their own miseries, Dorothy Dix went on dealing with the problems which beset others. She was able to understand youth even when it asked her to accept the viewpoint of a generation thrice removed from hers. She understood because her approach was always valid; she knew that there is no kindness greater, no charity more delicate, no advice more helpful than that which shows the mentally or spiritually or emotionally impoverished how to help themselves.

To be a good Samaritan takes far more wisdom and tact and understanding than the average self-appointed fairy godmother shows any sign of possessing. What calls itself philanthropy and takes a bow for its generosity may be so eager for self-aggrandizement that it forgets who actually is the object of its benefactions. It is really a dreadful thing to be the victim of unwelcome charity.

A few Aprils ago a friend of ours left home and took up his temporary residence in a quiet little village half a day's journey from his New York apartment.

It happened this way: Gregory Nevil and his Jessica were a happy couple and he adored his three rampaging youngsters, but Jess thought Greg ought to get away from her and "the kids" in order to make good at what she called "the chance of a lifetime." He was an unknown composer who played the piano in a night club in order to support his family. He sometimes got a chance to play his own stuff. That is how the successful playwright Clive Bradley came to hear it, and that is how one of Greg's tunes wove itself into a lyric for the operetta Clive had been urged to write. Before long Clive Bradley had a book, some good lyrics, a backer and a producer who had a theater. All that was needed was a composer, and Clive thought he had him! Greg was asked to compose the score for the Bradley operetta which had already involved itself with one of his tunes. Clive asked Greg if he thought he could submit the score for the first act by the first of June. Greg told Clive he could try; and that is how he came to leave his wife and children and go off to the little cottage Jess had wangled for a pittance and for six weeks.

"'*Nur wehr die Sehnsucht kennt*'—'None but the Lonely Heart,'" Jess quoted to her husband when he asked if the children couldn't go to her mother and she come north with him. "Some of the world's loveliest music was inspired by the composer's loneliness and longing. Schubert's for instance. And I hope you miss me enough to write another *Sehnsucht*—longing. Neither of us must break down until you're ready to come back with just the score your friend the playwright can show to his producer and backer. I'm sure this all-out sacrifice will make you and make your family's fortune."

The idea seemed sound—a working plan. But Greg and Jess figured without Isabel Radnor.

Mrs. Radnor was a buxom woman of sixty-five. Her own children had left home years before in order to escape her cloying idea of how to be a good mother. Now she lived alone in the large house behind the big hedge which Jessica had thought would assure Greg of privacy and peace.

Isabel's heart needed an object for its compulsive beneficence. When she became aware of the "lonely recluse" in the little house next to her big estate, she realized she had found her man. She prowled her grounds with no sense of snooping; she heard the tentative chords, the snatches of melody which came from the cottage; she yearned to do something for the lonely neighbor who had nothing but his piano. She couldn't bear the idea of his being helpless in that cottage without anyone to "do for him." She shivered at the thought of the cold April and the limited amount of wood stored on her neighbor's back porch. He just had to have more logs.

Before Greg had been in his haven of refuge for a full two days, Isabel Radnor had sent her yardman over to offer his help in cutting down some of the firewood trees on the back lot. The next day she baked bread, took Greg a loaf and assured him he would never be without fresh bread, because she baked twice a week and would not neglect him. The day after that she stopped by to say she was driving down to the village to do her marketing, and since the nice young man, who had begun to seem like a son already, didn't have a car she'd be glad to get his things for him.

Sunday she came by to offer to drive him to church. When on Monday he went out into the yard for a breath of air, the seemingly omnipresent Mrs. Radnor shouted through the hedge that she had a washing machine and would be glad to do his laundry and sew on his missing buttons. She'd seen from one of his letters, which had got into her mailbox by mistake, that he was Gregory Nevil, and since one of her sons was Gregory, too, she felt closer than ever to her neighbor. Wasn't he the Gregory Nevil who had married that pretty Jessie Smith about seven years back, and how was Jessie, and why wasn't she up here with her husband? Gregory had lost his breath long before Mrs. Radnor came to the end of hers. He said he had come up to the cottage to work and that Jessie was at home minding the children, while he concentrated on a job for which he had to have quiet and peace. Then he escaped. But not for long.

That night Mrs. Radnor invaded the cottage to bring Greg his dinner on a tray, and she sat down to visit with him while he ate it. She said it was a shame for him and his pretty wife to be separated and that she had figured a way to take care of that. She was driving down to New York tomorrow to get new specs, and when she came back the next day she would bring Jessie and their children up for the rest of his stay. The young ones could live in her house, and she would see that they were no care to their parents. That way Jessie could take real good care of him.

The next day, after Mrs. Radnor was on her way south, Greg indulged in an extravagant telephone call to New York.

"I can't work here," he said to Jess. "I haven't got even one single lyric set, and the libretto won't get going. There's a fairy godmother next door who's forever waving her wand under my eyes and singing her incantations in my ears, and that's all I can hear or see. She threatens to pick you and the children up in her car and transplant you all up here. Don't come. Don't budge. I can't work in the same atmosphere where this indomitable soul breathes forth her fire and sparks. Sit tight. I'll be home in the morning."

So Gregory Nevil left the Peace Cottage, on which he and Jessica had counted for inspiration, and he went back to his little apartment in the noisy city. And right there in the bedlam, which flowed around him without paying any special attention to him, he composed the successful score which was the first of his many triumphs.

Some of us, like Jessica and Gregory, fancy that we could produce a masterpiece of some kind if we had the right conditions for doing our work. Most of us can do our work wherever we are and in spite of the well-intentioned but destructive Isabel Radnors of our world. But we must seek in *ourselves* the means of sovereignty. We find our refuge from turmoil, our Peace Cottages, in the poised thought, the controlled approach which knows that ideas come from the source of ideas, the Creator, and can always be heard by the listening ear in spite of the din and tumult of the day.

Every one of us needs charity now and then: the tender, tolerant understanding which offers its gifts quietly, simply and without calling the world to witness how generous it is.

Every one of us needs to learn to live his own life as well as he knows how and to refrain from trying to live anyone else's life for him. It takes a lot of doing to understand one's self, to manage one's self, and to express one's self joyously and with just enough restraint and no self-condemnation. But one's real basic freedom is the freedom to be the man of God's creating and not to have imposed on one the ideas and ideals of somebody else.

My wise and understanding mother used to say—and this is as near as she ever came to intruding on her daughter's mental and spiritual privacy: "If I were you, dear, I'd get the habit of sitting down at my desk and going to work every day at a certain definite hour and, so, of establishing mental office hours for myself." "If I were you" was always the basis of her approach. She suggested; she did not command. She never said, "Do this!" or "Do that!" She gave wise counsel and advice when I asked it or seemed to be on the brink of a headlong precipice. But she advised her daughter even then as Eliphaz advised Job centuries ago:

> I would seek unto God, and unto God would I commit my cause:
> Which doeth great things and unsearchable; marvellous things without number . . .

But each of us must seek within his own consciousness his means of sovereignty. Each of us must establish through his own thought his right to "think God's thoughts after him." A beautiful sunset may give you a sense of infinity. The overwhelming power of the ocean may give it to me. Someone else may reach his highest awareness of the Deity through poetry. But the awareness that life is a vast symphony comes to each individual in the way he is best fitted to perceive it and receive it.

Many years ago, and before music spoke a language I could understand, I was taken to my first symphony concert. The greater part of the program was given over to Bach. To my untrained ear and unprepared thought his magnificent counterpoint sounded like mathematics, geometric progressions without warmth or beauty. I was bored by Bach and wished I could go home. But Fritz Kreisler was the soloist, and in the second half of that hitherto trying evening I found a beauty and satisfaction such as I had never before known anywhere but in church or the sanctuary of the spring woods. And yet, what the master's violin played was not churchly or magnificent music. It was the "Caprice Viennois" and the "Kamennoi Ostrow," whose very names speak of their color and gayety. An important critic wrote that the evening was spoiled by bad programming and that the two halves did not make an artistic whole nor present the great genius of the violin at his best. But for one in his audience the simple pieces he played opened the door to musical appreciation.

Beauty is indeed in the ear as well as in the eye of the beholder. We cannot force our ideal on someone else. The response to beauty lies in the heart of each individual man and woman and in the individual recognition of good which each feels through his own perceptions.

So after you and I learn what is to us our highest right, our supreme good, the answer to our prayers, we must learn also to let those we love find their own good, their own satisfaction, the answer to *their* prayers.

There is a very definite lesson in the story of the strident woman who took her shy little three-year-old daughter to the child's first party, planked the timid child down in a chair and said, "I brought you to this party to hev a good time, and you set there and hev it, durn you!"

That mother was an illiterate. But there is an illiteracy of the heart as well as of the head.

If you are an interfering husband or wife, or mother or father, or brother or sister, ask yourself if what you demand of Judy and Jerry is really as good for them as you claim or just good for your sense of being a superb guide and mentor.

Don't be a philanthropist at somebody else's expense. (This can't be said too often!) Don't be a tyrant however benevolent. And don't overlook the fact that imposed advice may be as frustrating to the giver as to the rebellious receiver.

To guard, guide and aid the immature, the sick, the lost is true kindness. To help the needy is charity. To protect the weak and straying is love. Such giving seeks to bless, not to impress. It offers what is needed, not what it needs to get out of its system.

Solomon writes in Proverbs: "... with all thy getting get understanding." True understanding is gentle. It entreats; it does not try to enforce. Once it has found within itself the means of sovereignty it is ready to allow to every man his sovereign right to find his way for himself and through divine guidance, for "they shall be all taught of God." (John 6:45.)

PART 3

REAL-*ization*

Learn to Cultivate Your Eternal Values

13

NO GIFTS FROM CHANCE

In the wide arena of the world, failure and success are not accidents as we so frequently suppose, but the strictest justice. If you do your fair day's work, you are certain to get your fair day's wage—in praise or pudding, whichever happens to suit your taste.

—ALEXANDER SMITH, *Dreamthorp*,
"On the Importance of a Man to Himself"

THE people who knock on wood when things are going well and laugh apologetically for their childishness are no more superstitious than those who greet desirable events with a shout of "This is much too good to be true!"

Why should anything be too good to be true? Wouldn't it be constructive to reverse the process and declare unhappy conditions too bad to be true?

Good is a positive force and the very essence of life. If it were otherwise, how could inexperienced, uninstructed primitive man have survived the somewhat terrifying phenomena of his evolving world? He was a stranger on a barren earth, and he had to cope with fire, flood, famine, drought and a number of other inhospitable material conditions. His survival indicates that "there is a spirit in man: and the inspiration of the Almighty giveth them understanding." (Job 32:8.)

In a recent baccalaureate address, called "The Myth of Defeat," George Channing, at that time editor of the Christian Science publications, told the graduating class of the University of California that every member of it was unbeatable if he would protect the integrity of his own thought.

Evil, unsupported by human acceptance, belief and consequent procedure, is impotent; and this is provable fact.

The story of Nehemiah illustrates dramatically and decisively how man can protect the integrity of his thought and purpose. During the period of the captivity, Nehemiah was cupbearer to the great Artaxerxes. When Nehemiah got news of the desperate condition of faraway Jerusalem, he longed to rebuild its crumbling walls in order that the city might be protected from its enemies. The great king recognized Nehemiah's dedication to his project and gave him not only encouragement but support. So Nehemiah set off for Jerusalem with high hopes, but enemies attacked him—and his idea—from every side.

From the beginning he had to deal with ridicule, treason, threats and chicanery. Sanballat the Horonite, Tobiah the Ammonite and Geshem the Arabian were the chief opponents of the rebuilding of the wall. They conspired to make Nehemiah abandon his work, but he refused to be deflected from the task which he felt had been given him by God. He inspired his co-workers with "a mind to work." And the project went ahead even when the laborers had to operate with weapons in one hand and tools in the other. Finally, in one last sly effort to trick Nehemiah, his enemies suggested that he come down to the villages of the plain for a conference. But his answer was: "I am doing a great work, so that I cannot come down: why should the work cease, whilst I leave it, and come down to you?"

Nehemiah was faithful to his task. He made much of it and nothing of the sly devices by which its opponents strove first to belittle and prevent it at its inception and then to destroy it at the very moment of its completion. In spite of the greedy mortgage rates imposed by native usurers, in spite of foreign attempts to intimidate, interfere or prevent the work from developing and the workers from persisting, the walls were rebuilt in the short space of fifty-two days. And the walls stood.

All this took place more than four hundred years before the coming of Jesus and his clear teachings about spiritual building. The truth he taught was always true, and men of good will and spiritual vision have always understood it in part and used it in proportion to their understanding. The wise and dedicated Nehemiah lived twenty-four hundred years ago, but his story is as modern as today. It can be translated without a hitch or an amendment into your experience and mine.

Anyone who "has a mind to work" (Nehemiah 4:6) must be prepared to defend his project against the enemies he objectifies in the external world and also against the traitors within his own sense of things. The builder finds himself beset by the temptation to think "I can't. . . . I never should have started this. . . . It is too much for me. . . ." and a host of equally discouraging and defeating suggestions. But he must not forget that they cannot become conditions of his experience unless he permits.

A poet sometimes finds a few lovely lines singing in his heart as spontaneously as the song of a bird. An exquisite refrain may sound over and over again in his thought. It comes to him because of the gift which makes him a poet. He has been given the beginnings of a poem, but he must labor to complete the structure. He must build a stanza at a time. He must search for the rhymes, the rhythms, to round out his inspiration from the brief bit of beauty which strayed into his thought or flowered out of it. So he hunts for an elusive word, for the *right* word, for the perfect phrase, for the sound that suits the sense and the note that uplifts it. And as he strives to "build his wall," to develop his inspiration into its full expression, his work may take on the plodding routine of drudgery. But if he is to make something of the beautiful moment when the inspired idea came to him, he must have a mind to work.

Inspiration may sound the first chords of a symphony. But the composer must work to find the rest of the notes!

It took Wagner more than ten years to compose the music and libretto of *Tristan and Isolde.* During those years he must often have had to deal with just such foes of achievement as have always attacked the Nehemiahs, the builders.

Sanballat and Tobiah and Geshem have existed through all times as the enemy; and as long as they are objectified as foes outside of consciousness, the alert are on guard against them, and the brave are stimulated by the challenge of actual conflict. But the sensitive have to deal with the enemy within: the fear of limitation, of perpetual bad luck, of inertia, of physical weakness or overwhelming weariness.

Deal with these foes in your own household firmly if you find them interfering with your work. There is no bad luck so stultifying as believing in luck. It deprives achievement of its tang. The unforeseen difficulty may be annoying, and the obstacle may be disheartening and disruptive; but there is always a way for the resourceful to cope with circumstance and for the temperamental to handle his own black moods. There is always a discoverable way around, through or over the barrier wall however high it looms.

It took only fifty-two days to rebuild the wall around Jerusalem. It took more than ten years to complete *Tristan and Isolde*. But they both got done, not by luck, or by chance, but by honest effort, by work and through that philosophy of faith which the wise include in their philosophy of life.

When a project is sound, a logical undertaking for you, an idea in which you have confidence, why should you not also have confidence in yourself, the one to whom the idea was revealed by creative intelligence? Revelation is inspiration. The listening ear hears it. The watchful eye see it. Inspiration does not come by chance, nor to those unprepared to receive it.

In the summer of 1949 the Reverend Samuel Henry Prince, the Canadian educator, began his thirtieth consecutive summer as guest pastor of St. Stephens Protestant Episcopal Church in New York City. His sermon included a declaration that those who claim life to be governed by chance are expressing what is little more than pagan philosophy. He called it disturbing that so much of modern education implies that chance is king. He expressed the conviction that his own colorful life was not governed by chance.

In 1919 Dr. Prince made his first trip from Canada to New York City. He wanted to take his doctor's degree at Columbia University. He was friendless and almost fundless in a strange city, but he was inspired to go to Dr. Nathan Seagle, then pastor of St. Stephens and in search of a part-time assistant.

Looking back over the years, who can believe that it was anything less than Divine Providence which opened the way for young Samuel Henry Prince to continue the educational course which he has put to such good use for humanity? It could not have been blind chance or luck which led him to the church, where he was preaching sanely and wisely and benignantly thirty years later.

Dr. Prince helped found the Maritime School of Social Work in Halifax, Nova Scotia; he became chairman of the Nova Scotia Housing Commission, president of the Interprovincial Reformatory for Women in New Brunswick, and professor of economics and sociology at King's College, Halifax.

Because he had no friends in the city to which he journeyed in his youth, because he had no funds, he knew at first hand what the problems of youth are and what poverty imposes. The limitations he was strong enough to surmount helped him to achieve the perception and tenderness which fitted him for the work he was to do and enabled him to bring to it the treasure of "a wise and understanding heart."

All through the ages the inspired thought has found the way through the Red Sea and the wilderness.

Inspiration is a bright flash of awareness soaring above and beyond the grooved thinking of the earth-bound day and its patterns. Inspiration parts the curtains of man's self-imposed sense of limitation; it offers a glimpse of the great possibilities, the divine potential, which preoccupation with material things hides from the worldly.

It is confidence in the potency of good, of wisdom and of an intelligent effort to express this power which inspires the great pioneers in science, art, exploration and theology and enables them to drive themselves beyond the outposts of accepted knowledge and into the field of the unknown. Such leaders have opened the way for all of us. In order to break the trail they had to defy tradition and deny superstition; and because they went forward in defiance of all the fears and doubts which tried to assail them, life is richer and fuller and freer for you and me. They labored beyond the despair front, the fatigue point and the danger zone. They defied popular opinion and renounced the creature comforts which all of us crave and cannot take along in a journey to an uncharted wilderness.

If you and I have need of renouncing the outworn but cozy and comfortable ways of yesterday, we must begin by lifting our concept of ourselves as being set in a groove and contented to stay there. Our world is full of people who have been forced out of their grooves and who have had to learn overnight to adjust themselves to strange patterns and terrains.

Last winter a New York hostess gave a reception which was made notable by the graciousness of the waitress who kept passing beautifully arranged trays of delicious sandwiches. The handsome, middle-aged woman in a maid's uniform was more of a hostess than the distrait party giver, who could not hide her vexation because her most distinguished guest, a world celebrity, had failed to appear. More concerned over the missing guest than over those who were on hand, the hostess did very little to make her tea a success. But the afternoon fairly glowed with the hospitality of the hired attendant.

Cups were never empty. Those who asked for coffee did not get tea with lemon; those who showed a preference for the shrimp or caviar sandwiches were not plied with hot meat hors d'oeuvres; those who said they would like *petits fours* rather than nut *torte* got cookies and not cake.

Later we learned that the waitress had been a famous hostess in Prague in the peaceful thirties. Now as a waitress-caterer at two dollars an hour she was making a living and sending her two small grandchildren to school. Their father, her son, had disappeared into the underground, through which he had tried to save his country from Hitlerism. The mother could not adapt herself to being a poor nobody in a strange land, and she slumped into invalidism and thus escaped responsibility. But the aristocratic grandmother discovered the thrill of pioneering. She triumphed in mastering the tasks she had once assigned to her staff of servants; and because her approach to making sandwiches and cakes and passing them to people who would once have been honored to visit her *Schloss* was confident and intelligent, she was able to maintain her dignity and poise in a so-called inferior position.

"Some day I'll have a little coffee shop," she said. "I am happy as I dream of it and work for it. The children must have their chance, you know."

The expectancy of a joyous tomorrow probably makes the heaviest tray that brave woman passes feel light to her willing hands. To know her is to realize anew the magnificence of the message in Psalm 90:

> Let thy work appear unto thy servants, and thy glory unto their children.
> And let the beauty of the Lord our God be upon us; and establish thou the work of our hands upon us; yea, the work of our hands establish thou it.

The story of Palissy, the potter, as dramatized in a play which the great English actor E. S. Willard brought to the United States at the beginning of this century is an example of that determination which persists in the face of every evidence of defeat. Bernard Palissy lived in Saintes, France, at the beginning of the sixteenth century, and was an undistinguished potter until he saw and fell in love with an antique white-enamel vase. Then he was inspired with a purpose and an ambition and a conviction that he could achieve. So he set out to discover the lost secret of the glaze which made that piece of porcelain so exquisite.

For a long time the secret eluded him, and his wife and children complained because he was not producing the stuff which bought them some few comforts. But Palissy persisted even when he had to burn the furniture of his poor studio in order to have wood enough to fire his kiln.

In the play's climactic scene, Palissy sat in front of his furnace, tired, worn, barely able to prevent himself from slumping to the ground from the one chair he had left. His wife berated him, his children cried for the sous he did not have to give them, and when he opened the door of his furnace he found nothing inside but a shapeless mass of sodden red clay. Then he burned his last possession; he broke the legs from his chair, tossed them into the furnace, and knelt in front of it to tend the flames.

I saw that play in my early childhood, but I have never been able to forget it.

All that was needed was that additional heat; that little

which was enough. The next time Palissy opened the door of his kiln he brought out a firm bowl, shining and beautiful.

How much of it happened just that way we cannot know. But history tells us that Bernard Palissy discovered the secret of a glaze which made him, the poor potter of Saintes, a famous master of ceramics and brought his family a comfortable way of living. The poor potter did not fail his dream.

If failure is not admitted to consciousness, how can it manifest itself in experience? To capitulate to defeat is to go down to self-destruction. But without someone to give them validity and to offer them an agency through which to operate, fear and defeat and discouragement are mere words—abstractions. So the man who has enough faith in his purpose to deny and defy discouragement and its taunts of failure shuts failure off at its source.

> I would seek unto God, and unto God would I commit my cause:
>
> Which doeth great things and unsearchable, marvellous things without number. . . .

Here, in the above lines from Job 5:8-9, we have a positive statement of an approach to life which does not ask and does not expect gifts from chance but knows that "except the Lord build the house, they labour in vain that build it. . . ."

There can be no gifts from chance because there is no

such thing as chance. It is nothing short of intellectual blindness and spiritual heresy to doubt that creative mind has a purpose and a plan, and that it is a good plan. The wise do not seek for a chance, an opportunity, with a timorous hope that fate will smile and be kind. Logic and reason unite to prove that all good gifts come from the unchangeable good, the creative, purposive, positive force called God. Recognizing this, men avail themselves of the fact that the gifts of intelligence are here for their taking, and that if they fail, it is for lack of directed, incessant and honest effort to succeed.

Mind's ideas are complete and whole even if revealed only in part. They are intended for fulfillment; they can be worked out. We stand in our own light, we block our own paths, we destroy our opportunities by refusing to recognize the basic fact that we were intended to succeed, equipped to achieve, and endowed with the ability to carry out the high purpose of creative mind.

We were not born to fail, but we actually persist in failing. William Wordsworth once wrote:

> Look for the stars, you'll say that there are none;
> Look up a second time, and, one by one,
> You mark them twinkling out with silvery light,
> And wonder how they could elude the sight!

It is that looking again which makes the master builder.

14

THE DURABLE SATISFACTIONS

Earth's crammed with heaven,
And every common bush afire with God;
And only he who sees takes off his shoes;
The rest sit round it and pluck blackberries.

—ELIZABETH BARRETT BROWNING,
"Aurora Leigh"

CHARLES ELIOT NORTON of Harvard University once told the Archaeological Institute of America that the outstanding distinction of the ancient Greeks may well have been their recognition of the indissoluble connection between beauty and goodness.

A line from the Apocrypha tells us to "Look upon the rainbow and praise him that made it." The state of consciousness which is enriched by beauty and inspired to give thanks for all the splendor of the common day cannot be touched by poverty.

The cold magnificence of a smoky winter sunset and the frail loveliness of the first timid leaves of spring bear witness to a creative power beyond and above all our science and art. None of us has ever held the south wind in his fist, but all of us have felt its mellow benediction. Those who sense the "dim beauty at the heart of things" are enriched by their awareness. The response to beauty frequently expresses itself with definite and tangible practicality in human affairs.

In the San Fernando Valley a woman's life was reorganized by her recognition of the potential in a patch of red and green and yellow gourds in her own yard. According to a newspaper story, this woman was faced with a sudden need to make a living for herself and her children. Her situation was a modern version of "what hast thou in the house?" (II Kings 4:2.) Not a pot of oil this time but a bright tangle of what some might have called weeds! The California woman had no conventional resources: no training, no capital, no experience. But she had an awareness of beauty, and her imagination was her working capital. She invested it in an idea, and she and her sons began carving whimsical little animals out of the bright-colored gourds in their yard.

Today she has a studio from which charming and original plant arrangements and decorative ornaments go to customers all over the country.

Even when it seems that beauty has no relation to the beholder, the wealth of the heart can be measured by its capacity to enjoy and to wonder.

Not so long ago I was walking down Madison Avenue in New York City with a woman I've known since kindergarten days. I stopped to look at some wonderful aquamarines glowing against velvet cushions behind the deep concavity of a plate-glass window, which brings its display so deceptively near. While I stood enchanted, Veronica marched away, her silver-blue mink cape repudiating window-shopping and window-shoppers.

When I caught up with her she demanded, "What's the point of gawking at anything in Y & Z's window? They charge for aquamarines as if they were diamonds!"

I said I valued aquamarines more highly than diamonds because of their wonderful color. I was trying to make Veronica smile at the idea. When she didn't react I added that the blue sky was much lovelier than the white clouds, and Veronica pounced on that.

"Rubbish!" she said. "Nobody in her right mind prefers aquamarines to diamonds. Anyway those monstrous stones are nothing for you. You couldn't carry them. They'd look absurd, and, besides, you can't afford Y & Z's prices, and you know it."

One grows accustomed to old friends and their too realistic frankness.

"I can afford to look," I said.

Veronica sniffed. "There's no point in looking at things you can't afford to own."

"Nobody expects to own a piece of the sky or part of the ocean, but everybody loves to look at them," I ventured to say.

"So what!" Then Veronica's mood changed. "I could hate you for making me think about those aquamarines. Blue is my color. If Charles hadn't forbidden me to charge another thing, I'd go back and see what aquamarine earrings and a necklace would do for my eyes. I'm getting to be such an old bag that if I don't have the right accessories to dramatize me, nobody notices me any more . . . not even Charles."

"You're still a handsome woman when you don't scowl so fiercely," I said. "Listen, honey: 'Deck thyself now with majesty and excellency; and array thyself with glory and beauty.' A smile will do more to make Charles notice you than aquamarines——"

"Fiddlesticks! And stop quoting poetry. I never cared for it."

"I was quoting from the Bible."

"Is that your idea of the place to look for beauty formulas?"

Veronica made an accusation of it, but she did not wait to see if I would defend my position. "Your aquamarines have ruined my day," she said. "I want them, and I don't dare get them. I can't have any of the things I crave any more. If I were still the glamour girl he married, Charles wouldn't be so stingy with me. He's cut my allowance, and I'm so miserably poor I can't even invite you to a decent place for tea."

So I invited her.

Veronica is poorer than she knows. She would have sniffed again if I had asked her to consider the meaning of that lovely line, "I am part of all I behold." But she did not sniff at the luxury of tea in a swank hotel.

The satisfaction which is derived from pride of ownership is limited at its source. Beauty is in the eye of the beholder. To be in tune with it, to be aware of it, is to know joy and satisfaction which the years cannot take away. There is inevitable poverty for the self-centered thought which cannot enjoy unless it possesses. It cannot own the lovely bird song which fades on the evening air, nor the glow of dawn, nor the rapture of any lovely moment. There never was any security in material possessions and dependence on them.

Yesterday's peach-blossom skin will no more see a woman through middle age than yesterday's bank account will take care of next year's debts. When the sharp edge of a Veronica's beauty is dulled, she can still hold her own if her wit is mellow and her heart is generous.

It is what the world calls the intangibles which last. The fruits of mind and spirit do not decay. Moth and rust cannot destroy them. To be convinced of the power and presence of good is to make it operative in experience. To believe in the enduring quality of beauty and truth and grace is not to dream in a realm of fantasy; it is to be wide awake to spiritual perfection and gratefully aware of the immortality of the things of spirit.

The confident sense that beauty and good exist, persist and are always present for you to grasp, express and enjoy will enable you to REAL-ize the ever-present perfection you have conceived as true and desirable and attainable.

All that expresses good in action is the result of a state of consciousness and not a set of circumstances.

The lasting, durable, reliable satisfactions of our lives grow out of what each of us makes of self, not from what we let conditions and events make of us. You and I must cultivate our ability to appreciate and be grateful for every little bit of beauty or grace we glimpse; we must form the habit of bringing beauty and grace into all our relationships. As Voltaire wrote in *Candide:* "Let us cultivate our garden." If there isn't a garden in our hearts, we won't see the full loveliness of the garden in our yards. Perhaps the ground in the yard next door is richer. Perhaps they have a gardener. But we must work with what we have and love it into loveliness.

Real values are not easy to determine. Old Judge Dixon used to tell the story of the crate of oversize, pale-skinned citrus fruit one of his clients sent him from Florida years before grapefruit had been incorporated into the breakfast menu of the average home.

"The wife and I sneered at that miserable gift," he would say with a chuckle. "We looked at those big green 'oranges' and decided they weren't worth houseroom. We thought an orange ought to be orange-colored, not a pale lemony yellow. I felt sure such outsize fruit was bound to be woody, so I put the box into the woodshed, and the client who had sent me such a gift went into the mental doghouse. But one day the wife fetched in a couple of those palefaces and cut them in two for spooning out at Sunday breakfast. We all thought them mighty sour, but one of my kids was resourceful enough to sugar his, and first thing you knew we were all smacking our lips and figuring if we oughtn't to spare a few for the folks next door."

The world keeps learning the value of things once fully as suspect as Judge Dixon's grapefruit. But if we put the untested and untried into the woodshed and don't take the trouble to get acquainted with the unknown, we are likely to miss out on some very pleasant discoveries.

All prejudgments indicate a lack of judgment. To dismiss an idea, a theory, a thing or a situation as uninteresting because one has not had enough interest in life itself to investigate is to shut oneself off from more knowledge, more opportunity and more growth. How can one find the answer without knowing and studying the problem? The Veronicas may refuse to learn, and the Judge Dixons don't always have investigating wives. As for you and me, let us open our eyes, our minds and our hearts. Let us acquaint ourselves with the truth of what is going on around us. Let us go farther and "acquaint now thyself with him, and be at peace. . . ."

15

CHOOSE LIFE!

As the marsh-hen secretly builds on the watery sod,
Behold I will build me a nest on the greatness of God:
I will fly to the greatness of God as the marsh-hen flies
In the freedom that fills all the space twixt the marsh and the skies:
By so many roots as the marsh-grass sends in the sod
I will heartily lay me a-hold on the greatness of God.

—SIDNEY LANIER, "The Marshes of Glynn"

RIGHT where you are is where God is. That statement should not shock or startle you. It is implicit in much of what has already been said in these pages. The fact it records has been proved through faith by many of the spiritual leaders of the past; and in the next chapter we shall see that the scientists of our day are proving it by formula and equation.

Most of us humans learn as we go, and by the trial-and-error method. So it is not surprising to find that Moses, the great Hebrew leader, was once a worldly and violent man who had to be chastened and developed by a desert experience before he was ready for his lifework and prepared to lead a people out of bondage. That brief summary of one of the greatest careers of all times might well be applied to any man's career. The strong and good not only survive the wilderness but come out of it wise, gracious, tolerant, humble and filled with an understanding gained in the solitude of their desert journey.

By the time Moses was prepared to receive the Ten Commandments he had advanced to the point of spiritual perception where he knew that God was not a far-off Deity, enthroned beyond the sky, but was the ever-present "I AM" who would never fail those who turned to Him for guidance. Moses yearned to share his vision with his people; so he told them:

> I call heaven and earth to record this day against you, that I have set before you life and death, blessing and cursing: therefore choose life, that both thou and thy seed may live:
>
> That thou mayest love the Lord thy God, and that thou mayest obey his voice, and that thou mayest cleave unto him: for he is thy life, and the length of thy days. . . .

Jesus exceeded Moses in spiritual understanding; he saw that "I and my Father are one." He did not have any sense of separation from his Maker, such as that which kept Moses from entering his Promised Land.

To forget or ignore the basic truth that mind is always present and ever powerful is to be in some degree shut out from wisdom and its promptings. (See Job 23:13, Romans 11:33-34, I Corinthians 2:16, Philippians 2:5.) To be aware that God is a God at hand is to be prepared to meet any emergency. Sometimes truth is learned by indirection. But whether it is in the wilderness or on a cross, humanity does not seem ready for truth until it has suffered from its own belief in evil.

It was through an experience which threatened to destroy their faith in good, and even in God, that a group of young folk learned an unforgettable lesson.

For many years a number of congenial families had spent their summers at a quiet northern resort where a well-known religious conference met annually. The children at Lake M. grew up in a simple, prayerful, but by no means sanctimonious atmosphere. They had happy normal vacations, and the leader in most of their good times was Hilda. She was a graceful, pretty girl, liked by the older folk, loved by her own group and adored by the younger boys and girls.

One July night there was a sudden squall on the lake. It was the worst midsummer storm anyone could remember in that region, and it left death in its wake. The next morning Hilda's sailboat was found capsized at the far end of the lake with her body entangled in the rigging. The mast was snapped off short, the mainsail was rolled over her head and the ropes were twisted around her arms.

It seemed incredible that Hilda should have been drowned in the lake over which she had presided so gaily. She was one of the best swimmers in that part of the country. She had learned to sail when she was a small child and had been winning cups in yacht races ever since she was old enough to enter them. But there was no hint of foul play in her death unless it was on the part of the Deity, who—as all the young folks felt—had failed their lovely Hilda and was, therefore, no longer to be trusted.

There was a painful problem in theology involved in the drowning. The youngsters at the lake rebelled when a few stern religionists tried to convince them that Hilda had been punished for disobeying her mother, who had always begged her not to sail alone at night. The children were equally opposed to the smug orthodoxy which suggested that she had been an angel, and so God had taken her to Himself. All those teen-agers who had loved the older girl grew restive and bitter that summer, disobedient to authority and rebellious against a God who had permitted such a cruel thing to happen to their Hilda. Finally an old sailor who had taught Hilda how to handle a boat set himself to renew their faith.

"Our Hilda didn't keep her head that night," he told the young rebels. "The squall gave plenty of warning before it turned into a big blow. I was down to the inlet where it struck the hardest, and I had plenty of time to get into safe harbor. Hilda had her chance to jump clear and swim to shore if she was a mind to. If she'da taken a few seconds to ask God what to do, He'd told her not to try to reef sail in that wind. God didn't have a thing to do with drowning our friend. She wasn't having any dealings with God that night but only with that boat she come near worshiping. She wouldn't want any of you kids to be holding God accountable for what He woulda warned her not to do if she'd consulted Him. As I figure it, she'd want all of you to remember that God will show you the way if you ask Him to. She'd want you to learn something from her, so she wouldn't have died for nothing. And this is what I think Hilda left you as her last words: 'Listen, kids. Learn from me and what I didn't do, and never forget that you can always hear God's voice over the biggest kind of a blow if you listen for it and let him steer your boat.' "

In human experience there are storms on land as well as on water, and they who let God steer their craft can weather the storms. Some unhappy few do not know that there is a power to which they can turn. Some are too arrogant to look beyond their own resources. Some let fear mesmerize them, cloud their judgment and black out their ability to see clearly and act intelligently. They are the victims of their own misperception and misconception and not of the storm to which poised, confident thought can learn to say its "Peace be still!"

Panic can never take possession of the thinking of anyone who has learned to stand on the fact that God is the only lawmaker. It is written in Psalm 27:1:

> The Lord is my light and my salvation; whom shall I fear? the Lord is the strength of my life; of whom shall I be afraid?

If you fill your heart with such awareness of God, how can you lose your head?

One who looks clear-eyed and confident at any situation, however fearsome it may appear to be, gains the reasoning and reasonable perspective which is bound to reveal just how to cope with the problem at hand. The panic-stricken gaze is not clear enough to see the way of escape, but mind sees and can reveal it.

In the fall of 1929 a woman in a large Eastern city found herself stripped of everything she had been taking for granted. When her husband committed suicide after a tragic business crash, Charlotte felt that her heart, her courage, and her life had been destroyed. She and her children had to move out of a twenty-room mansion into a single room in a cheap boardinghouse.

She did not know how she was going to maintain even that shabby refuge after she had exhausted the money raised from the sale of her personal possessions. She had no near relatives. Her onetime friends were now her creditors, and some of them had been impoverished by her husband's stock-market manipulations; so she could ask for nothing from them. Charlotte was humiliated, brokenhearted and helpless. She was tempted to take her husband's way out and commit suicide. But she could not bring herself to take her seven-year-old twins with her, and she could not leave them alone in what she now saw as a hostile world.

In her black despair Charlotte went to a wise and spiritual-minded woman, Mrs. Hadley, who had once been her Sunday-school teacher and her ideal. Charlotte's marriage, her husband's growing wealth and prominence and his liking for stimulating company had swept her into a busy sphere where she had no time for Mrs. Hadley. For years Charlotte had not thought of her former teacher except as a sweet old thing to whom she loved sending lavish gifts at Christmas and Eastertide. Now she was astonished when the gentle counselor to whom she had turned, because there was nowhere else to go, did not offer her sympathy or commiseration but pounced on her sternly.

"Stop being so sorry for yourself!" Mrs. Hadley demanded. "Don't get cross-eyed from staring at yourself surrounded by problems. You'll never stare your troubles down if you do. And stop whimpering over the past. Save your voice to call up a future."

Charlotte was offended. She got up to leave, but Mrs. Hadley did not rise with her. "Walk out on me if you choose," she said. "But can you walk out on your problem? Won't you have to take it along with you?"

Charlotte choked. "I didn't come here to be scolded. I expected a little human sympathy from you. The Ann Hadley I remembered had something of the Christ spirit."

"Jesus rebuked error."

Charlotte sat down. It was as if a firm but gentle hand had pushed her back into her chair.

"It looks as if you might be ready to take your attention off yourself and turn it to God," Mrs. Hadley said.

Charlotte began to cry. She had not dared cry till that moment. "But I've got to find a way to take care of Janey and Johnny, and there just isn't any way. I'm not trained for any job. I've no influential friends to give me one. Actually I don't see why anyone should give me a chance. I guess they think I was extravagant and demanding and egged poor Nick on——"

" 'Let the government be on his shoulder,' " Mrs. Hadley said gently. "That text is elaborated in the ninth chapter of the Book of Isaiah. Read it later on. Right now what you need to do is turn your attention from the handicaps and incapacities you've been dwelling with, and focus it on God's infinite capacity. 'In my Father's house are many mansions,' Jesus said. And one of them is prepared for you. There's a place for you, waiting for you, Charlotte. Or do you think the Bible is a pack of lies?"

"Why no!" Charlotte said, startled by the idea. "But I don't see what it's got to do with the situation. It doesn't tell me what to do, and I've got to do something. I've nothing left to sell but my engagement ring. When that's gone what's to become of Johnny and Janey? I'll have nothing——"

"You'll still have *you,*" Mrs. Hadley said. "I wish you'd start looking to God as confidently as your Johnny and Janey look to you. Aren't you good for anything but making minus signs?"

It astonished Charlotte to hear herself laughing. "I've always been considered a good hostess. I never had any trouble training servants. Maybe I could *be* one. I'm willing to scrub floors if it pays. But I can't think who would hire me without a reference or who would give me one."

"You said you were a good hostess." Mrs. Hadley fairly pounced on it. "I know a woman who has a delightful tearoom at the state capital. I also know she needs a hostess who will be able to get on with her staff and the state senators and representatives who eat there every day. And she needs a hostess who looks the part. I'm your reference and hers too. I think Ellen McClintock will be glad to make a place for you and the children in her big, lonely house. . . . Life's a difficult jig-saw puzzle, Charlotte, till you see how to fit the parts together. Yesterday Ellen McClintock brought me her piece of the puzzle. Today yours comes in, and it fits perfectly. I've been expecting as much——"

"How could you?" Charlotte began impatiently. And then her thought and her voice changed. "I didn't expect anything when I came here. But I had nowhere else to go."

"You were led to come here today——"

"Led? You believe God brought me here, don't you? But I can't believe there's such a simple solution to my complicated problem." Charlotte laughed, uneasily this time. "It's almost too pat!"

"No, it's just perfect." Mrs. Hadley smiled with gentle assurance. "What I feel sure is going to work out for you and Ellen McClintock is another proof—and I've seen many—of my beloved Bible verse, 'Before they call, I will answer; and while they are yet speaking, I will hear.' Now I'll telephone Ellen and see how soon she can come to town and talk to you, or if she wants you to come to the capital, sight unseen."

Charlotte has grandchildren now. Some of you who have motored through New England have probably eaten at the lovely country inn she owns and still enjoys supervising. She likes to tell the story of how good began operating in her experience as soon as she gave it a chance.

Nobody can whistle a gay roundelay while permitting a dirge to toll in his head. Nobody can advance while concentrating on retreat. When Job declared that the thing which he greatly feared had come upon him, he was stating a basic psychological fact: Our fears are bullies as well as braggarts; they take advantage of every opening we permit them to find; they lay claim to having more power than good itself; and if we admit their claim, they have a chance of establishing themselves as valid.

An inspiring Old Testament story is that of how Jehoshaphat and the tribe of Judah were terrified when they heard that the children of Moab and the children of Ammon and mount Seir were coming against them in battle array. Jehoshaphat turned to God in prayer, acknowledging humbly that he and his people had "no might against this great company that cometh against us; neither know we what to do: but our eyes are upon thee." (II Chronicles 20:15-17.) Then Jahaziel, a Levite, was inspired by the spirit of the Lord, and he said: "Be not afraid nor dismayed by reason of this great multitude; for the battle is not yours, but God's. Tomorrow go ye down against them. . . . Ye shall not need to fight in this battle: set yourselves, stand ye still, and see the salvation of the Lord with you, O Judah and Jerusalem: fear not, nor be dismayed . . . for the Lord will be with you." And when the next day came, Judah and Jerusalem went to battle with a song of praise to God in their hearts and on their lips. They had confidence and unity, but the enemy fell out among themselves. "For the children of Ammon and Moab stood up against the inhabitants of mount Seir, utterly to slay and destroy them. . . ."

One of the wisest women I know has a habit of saying, "Let go; let God." That is today's version of the word which came to Jehoshaphat's men. When spiritual inspiration is allowed to take possession of thought, it will guide action.

Do you find any trace of logic or consistency in declaring the might and majesty of the Creator and denying the allness of that supreme power? Is there anything to be gained by expecting defeat, any chance of attacking a problem effectively and wholeheartedly if you don't expect to win? Can you reasonably expect the goodness of God to operate for you or through you unless your faith in it opens a channel in your own thought through which it can be expressed?

We make our own defeat inevitable by shutting ourselves off from the source of success. Our failure to invoke and follow the leadings of "that mind which was also in Christ Jesus" is the only failure there can ever seem to be. The Bible record, and the record of our own experience, offer enough proof to establish the fact of a power, presence, wisdom and government at work in our universe and functioning on a basis of law above and beyond any man-made statutes. When and as our laws are derived from and kept in harmony with this divine law, the government of good protects, guides and inspires us. When we turn to this law and open the doors of consciousness, so it can come in and operate, we find our little cosmogonies running smoothly and with a harmony such as the strongest human determination of which we are capable will never produce.

After you and I have witnessed the results of our own faith often enough, we are bound to trust the All-Powerful and to acknowledge that it is always ready to act if invoked understandingly and with full confidence. But good does not force itself through closed doors, nor into the thought which is barred against it. So it is not difficult to understand that whatever appears to exist outside the jurisdiction of the Almighty God is and must be a figment of the human imagination. It has only the substance of our fancy or dream. When and as we wake up and stop dreaming and supporting our dream—or nightmare—what becomes of it?

The prophet Habakkuk wrote: "Thou art of purer eyes than to behold evil, and canst not look on iniquity. . . ." And how can what God does not see have any possible semblance of reality if you and I don't insist that it has?

When we recognize that whatever comes into experience comes as thought and through our acceptance of it, we see the wisdom of being very selective about what we admit into our consciousness, which is our house of life. Let us refuse with growing assurance to allow unwelcome thoughts to make themselves at home in this house of ours and so gain strength to manifest themselves as facts in experience.

Learning to play the violin, to speak a new language, or to understand and apply the laws of mathematics is a matter of self-discipline, study and practice. Nobody ever said, "Abracadabra! I will now write a great lyric poem," and produced it without further effort. Nobody establishes his thinking and his life on a sound, working basis without a process of seeking, study and growth. There are three steps we must all take in order to gain true spiritual understanding and its inevitable and outstanding rewards. These steps are:

First: Establish our philosophy of life on the recognition that God, good, *is* and is *all:* all-powerful, ever-present and ever-operative.

Second: Obliterate from our thinking any vestige of belief in another—and malicious—power working in opposition to God, good.

Third: Accept and contemplate the fundamental truth that God, in the very nature of His being as cause, the Creator and law is always positive, never negative; always creative, never destructive; always the producer of growth, never of decay or destruction.

When by these three steps in the thought realm you arrive at the realization that God is life, good, perfection, law and mind, you have a magnificent array of proof of your simple creed: God *is.* God is good. God has no opponent. And then it is easy to know that " . . . God hath not given us the spirit of fear; but of power, and of love, and of a sound mind."

In an article in *Reader's Digest* Paul de Kruif wrote with clear perceptiveness about modern methods of dealing with one of the great scourges of our times: alcoholism. He told of the magnificent work done by Alcoholics Anonymous and how that movement came into existence. Its founder had struggled with the drink habit for years. It came to him in a hospital that he could not by himself conquer the pestilential enemy that was wrecking his health and his career. He saw that he would have to recognize a power for good bigger than himself and that he would have to turn to that power for strength to do what he had never been able to do on his own. Then he proved his dominion over the appetite which was undermining his life. So, actually, the great achievements of Alcoholics Anonymous, like that of the greatest humanitarian and healing agencies of all time, are based on the words Jesus spoke centuries ago: "I can of mine own self do nothing," and "the Father that dwelleth in me, he doeth the works."

The Father, the Creator, is expressed through His creation. As you and I cultivate the desire and the latent ability to be agencies for good (and good alone!) we become receptive to the power and presence of creative mind. As we respond to this power we become increasingly able to express it and to banish the bad habits of thinking which have brought about bad habits of living, whether they be sin or sickness, bodily ill or mental evil, or drunkenness.

There is a technique of the heart as well as of the head. We learn to use it through humble alertness, through active listening for inspiration, through honest open-mindedness, through wise selection of the basis on which to build our lives.

Good will be objectified and expressed in your experience and mine in the precise degree in which it is REALized in our thinking. It is ours to "refuse the evil, and choose the good." (Isaiah 7:15.) Nothing but our own folly can keep us from the course Moses recommended: ". . . choose life, that both thou and thy seed may live. . . ." (Deuteronomy 30:19.)

Archibald MacLeish has declared this simple truth for us and for our day in a single line: "The world was always yours; you would not take it."

But let us "choose life" aware that the good of the world is ours for the taking.

16

NOW IS FOREVER

Nothing shall be to come, and nothing past,
But an eternal now shall ever last.

—PETRARCH, "The Triumph of Eternity"

THE above lines were written in the fourteenth century. They bear witness to the continuity of thought which links all ages. When the apostle Paul was trying to persuade the Athenians that God was understandable, at hand, and by no means the mysterious unknown God to whom they had built an altar on Mars' Hill, he told them: "For in him we live, and move, and have our being; as certain also of your own poets have said. . . ."

Paul did not lack persuasive arguments of his own nor words to convey his ideas, but he knew that the debate-loving Athenians would be impressed by his ability to support his thesis with statements made by their own countrymen. So he quoted a line from Epimenides, and then fortified it with a phrase from the *Phaenomena* of Aratus.*

Mental clannishness is a world-old thing; so is scorn of the unfamiliar. Men accept new ideas more readily when these ideas arrive with letters of introduction.

But what, actually, is a new idea? And where shall we find one without roots in the past?

Moses startled the thought of his followers with his declaration: "Hear, O Israel: the Lord our God is one Lord. . . ." That may have sounded radical to a group of ex-slaves newly escaped from Egyptian bondage; but more than four centuries before, Abram, born about 1996 B.C. in Ur of the Chaldees, became aware of the one true God and worshiped Him.

In Exodus 15:18, at the beginning of the Old Testament, and in Revelation 11:15, at the end of the New Testament, both Moses and John use the statement that God shall reign for ever and ever. And those who heard John were amazed by his "new doctrine," although the existence of a ruling power had been declared again and again by prophet and seer, by Jew and Greek. But each generation and each nation and people discovered it anew, on its own terms and in its own language.

Midway in the fifteen centuries between Moses and the apostle John, the prophet Isaiah foretold the coming of

* My authority for this and subsequent statements concerning the Greeks is John A. Dakes's *Christ Jesus: The Authentic Story of the Founder of Christianity as Told by Matthew, Mark, Luke and John in the Four Gospels* (Chicago: The Avalon Publishing Company, 1940). Mr. Dakes was born of Greek parents on the Isle of Crete and has drawn from the Greek texts for his references to the Greek philosophers and poets.

the Messiah, and he called this messenger "the Word of God." John uses this same term in the Fourth Gospel; and what John called "the Word" was named "Logos" by the Greeks, as they in their turn caught their individual—and seemingly original—glimpse of the eternal truth for which there is no yesterday or tomorrow because it is always true. But truth always comes as a revelation to those who find out that their universe is spiritually mental, made up of ideas and concepts rather than of matter. And truth comes in just this fashion to you and to me, as if nobody had ever known it before and as if this moment, this *now* of ours, had rolled back the clouds of mythical beliefs so our individual and personal revelation of God's power and presence could shine through.

Five centuries before the birth of Jesus, Anaxagoras, the teacher of Pericles, discerned what he called an Agency or mind. He conceived of this Agency as independent of the material world, as possessed of all knowledge and power, and as ruling over all forms of life. So in the height of "the glory that was Greece" a great scholar made very much the same discovery as that which had come to the simple Abram of Chaldea.

Many of the Attic philosophers had their individual glimpses of what they called Reason expressing itself in the world, even as Reason of a lesser sort expressed itself in the conduct of men. Socrates used the arguments of Reason to arrive at the truth of being, which he named "The Idea of God." The Greeks found the teachings of Socrates menacing to the comfortable order of things as they were; so they decreed that he must drink the cup of hemlock and die. But his teachings marched on because they had always been some part of man's awareness and were perceived anew in the *now* of each succeeding age. In his *Republic* Plato, the foremost disciple of Socrates, quotes his teacher as saying, "...and the good is to be attributed to God alone; of the evils the causes are to be sought elsewhere, and not in him."

Socrates lived four centuries before Jesus; but his uplifted thought glimpsed some of the great facts of being which have always existed and go right on existing whether they are recognized or not.

Spiritual truth has gone shuttling like a bright thread through the dingy pattern of the ages. But because it is always reborn in the light of its own reappearing, it is always fresh and new to those who are ready to be enlightened by it. Because tyranny, greed and orthodoxy are unwilling to have the light of understanding turned on them, Socrates was accused of corrupting his students and was forced to drink the cup of poison, and Jesus was called a dangerous fellow and nailed to the cross. But the truth, which tyranny is always determined to suppress, can never be destroyed. It is constantly resurrected in the hearts of men.

As we have seen, this eternal, spiritual truth has been glimpsed again and again as the thought of man progressed. It has been called by many names—Agency, Logos, Reason and the Word are some of them—but whatever men of vision named their concept of divine power, their recognition of it grew out of a perception, however faint, of that which Jesus fully understood and proved in its entirety. And now, today, you and I can manifest this power in our lives in the degree that we "Let this mind be in [us] you, which was also in Christ Jesus." But the barriers we set up between ourselves and omnipotent good are exactly like those which divided the children of Israel from their heritage and kept them out of their Promised Land thousands of years ago in the *now* of which Moses was conscious.

We prattle about a God who is ever-present, all-powerful and forever beneficent; and in the degree that we believe it we shall see it manifested: "According to your faith be it unto you." We complain of lack of limitation; but the actual lack from which we suffer is lack of faith.

In every *now* those whose confidence in the truth they have glimpsed is wavering and uncertain are given to making themselves a Golden Calf, as the followers of Moses also did, because of a desire for a tangible something to worship. In the age-old continuity of human experience and human opinion about that experience we seem to be going through the same world-shaking situations our ancestors met when their time was the present and Attila the Hun or Goliath of Gath was their Hitler or their Stalin; for there is "One Universe made up of all that is; and one God in it all, and one Principle of Being, and one Law, the Reason shared by all thinking creatures, and one Truth."

Doesn't that sound modern? And so it is, since it expresses an idea far in advance of some of today's thinking. It was written by the Roman emperor Marcus Aurelius in the second century of the Christian Era.

The promise of the future lies in the record of the past. There was once a Pharaoh, of a line of Pharaohs; and his pitiless taskmasters stood ready to lash a man or a hundred men to death so the Pyramids might be built to the glory of the ruler of Egypt. There is always a Pharaoh, a symbol of tyranny; but the Moses-consciousness is invariably at hand to lead the despot's slaves out of bondage. And the ever-present spirit of the truth which inspired Moses and Jesus is still present and available to lead us out of the misery and poverty and sickness and sin which hold us in slavery. As Paul told the Ephesians over nineteen centuries ago there is "One Lord, one faith, one baptism, one God and Father of all, who is above all, and through all, and in you all."

As recently as the past century, but still in that "eternal now" where past and present meet, William James concluded an address given at Harvard to the Young Men's Christian Association with these words: "Be not afraid of life. Believe that life *is* worth living, and your belief will help create the fact." The entire address is included in William James's volume of essays, *The Will to Believe,* and its title is "Is Life Worth Living?" Almost three thousand years, as measured by our human sense of time, lie between William James and the writer of Proverbs. But in the eternal now with which mind bridges the centuries Solomon expressed the same truth when he wrote:

> Keep thy heart with all diligence; for out of it are the issues of life.

Truth is always "true"; it is never outmoded, dated, and never so new and radical that it cannot find recognition and acceptance in the hearts of those who seek the light. So don't be afraid to pioneer for spiritual enlightenment in your family, your community, your city, your state.

> Listen to the Exhortation of the Dawn!
> Look to this Day!
> For it is Life, the very Life of Life.
> In its brief course lie all the
> Verities and Realities of your Existence;
> The Bliss of Growth,
> The Glory of Action,
> The Splendour of Beauty.
> —"The Salutation of the Dawn"
> (translated from the Sanskrit)

17

THE KEYS OF HEAVEN

And wisdom and knowledge shall be the stability of thy times . . .
—Isaiah 33:6

In the course of their investigations of the cosmos natural scientists have recently arrived at some conclusions which support what students of the Bible have discerned through a thoughtful study of the first chapter of Genesis.

A few years ago the great English astronomer Sir Arthur Eddington stated that "Mind is the first and most direct thing in our experience; all else is remote inference."

In his Rede Lecture at the University of Cambridge the late Sir James Jeans, who was also an astronomer of note, though better known for his work in mathematics, said, "The universe begins to look more like a great thought than a great machine." On another occasion Sir James was quoted as declaring: "Everything which exists is the thought of the great Mathematician who is also the Architect of the Universe."

In today's world we do not have to be satisfied with

mere belief in God, however satisfying such a simple faith may be. We can prove God; and it is becoming evident to all sincere and conscientious investigators of basic truth that God is intellect or mind and that the control of mind's creation must be in the mental realm.

Admit that everything which exists is the creation—or expressed thought—of the governing mind, and it follows that man is an embodied thought or idea expressing mind. This conclusion is neither so new nor so radical as it may at first appear. It does not exceed the Bible statement: "And God said, Let us make man in our image, after our likeness: and let them have dominion over . . . every creeping thing that creepeth upon the earth." (Genesis 1:26.) It does not seem unreasonable to suppose that man continues to exist in the likeness of the creative mind which made him and that he retains his dominion over the sly and insidious doubts and fears which suggest themselves to him from time to time.

Most assuredly the scientific thinkers are not sentimentalizing when they claim that there is plan and purpose evident in the universe, that all which exists has its being as a result of this plan, and that the plan itself comes from a universal mind. The religious thinkers cannot go beyond that claim. They merely abide by it and regulate their lives by it. They accept the fact that "a system of things out of which Mind arose must be mental at bottom." They prove their thesis by living it, much as Albert Einstein proved his theory of relativity by working it out through equation and formula.

But even now the old-fashioned materialist clings to his false gods. He is no more ready to accept the idea that man is mind expressed and thought embodied than the Roman who worshiped Jove was ready to accept the spiritual teachings of Jesus. The materialist says, "The world I know is made up of things I can taste and touch and see. As long as I'm walking around on earth, how can I be expected to believe in anything of which my eyes and ears don't tell me? No spiritual intangibles for me. I don't hold with any of that moonshine. 'Embodied thought' indeed! What in the name of common sense is that? And how can a flesh-and-blood human being think of himself as 'an idea expressing Mind'? If you pinch me, I feel it. I'm a realist. Don't expect me to go along with any of your esoteric notions. And when a plain man like me puts them in his realistic way, don't you see how fantastic they are?"

How can we answer him more simply than with a few plain questions of our own? "Come, Mr. Realist, would you consider it esoteric or fantastic to call a statue an objectification of its sculptor's concept of what he can carve out of a log of wood or a block of stone? Didn't the Empire State Building have to be *thought* before it could be *wrought?* Did not the Triborough Bridge begin as an idea? Was not that magnificent structure over which thousands travel every day a mere figment of the imagination at its inception? Could you have touched it, or smelled it, or seen it, or crossed it then?"

Every structure is an idea before it becomes a span over a river, or a tower to the sky, or a vast housing project. A picture painted on canvas, a drama presented on the stage of a theater, a book between covers, and a symphony score orchestrated for a hundred musicians has an "isness" even when it is no more than a faint glimmer of inspiration in the thought of its author, painter, producer or composer. Each of these art products existed as an idea before it was advanced to the stage where you and I could see it, applaud it or deride it according to our standard of what is good and enjoyable, or of what is dull and meretricious.

The sewing machine and the electric mixer, the steam engine and the harvester are theories brought to fulfillment, ideas expressed in material form. It is granted that they are now material mechanisms—machines. But wasn't each an entity in the inventor's thought before it was materialized?

It has been said that man must learn to think God's thoughts after Him. This cannot be put more impressively than in the words of Psalm 46: "Be still, and know that I am God. . . ."

Sir James Jeans once said that the compulsion to invent mathematical symbols came from an inner necessity of man's mind. Man did not have to devise those symbols; he wanted to. No taskmaster stood over him with a whip and "beat the digits and the decimal system out of him." Man invented mathematical symbols because he had need of threes and fours and plus and minus signs to work with.

Man found a way to represent numbers and square roots and fractions, but he did not originate the principles of mathematics. He merely reasoned out its laws and how to use them. He is not personally responsible for those laws or their enforcement, but he must abide by them if he wants to work out his problems and get the benefit of the fair, just and unchanging rules of addition or subtraction.

In mathematics, as in any exact science, "Mind is the first and most direct thing in experience" and in operation.

Inevitably, in spite of anything you or I can do about it, one half of twelve is six and will always be six. None of our calculations will come out right if we insist that five plus five equal twelve. No one can work successfully in any field unless he learns and applies the rules for procedure in that field. And no one can live successfully without recognizing and utilizing the laws of life and the government of mind.

Mind is the highest form of expression of which we are conscious or have evidence. Whether we are working in science, the arts, philosophy, economics or government we must apply intelligence to everything we consider and every problem we attempt to work out. And intelligence derives from mind and expresses it. Mind creates and governs the world of ideas and the business of working out a way of life as well. Mind is supreme and a manifestation of God.

The day has passed when the agnostic or atheist can command respect by questioning or repudiating what one confessedly does not understand and what the other can deny but not disprove.

The spiritual-minded have come to have "faith in the

constancy of the divine purpose and the unvarying nature of God's laws," as the noted English preacher and suffrage leader Maude Royden puts it. Scholar, scientist and philosopher have proved what the religionist claims. In his book, *The Universe and Dr. Einstein,* Lincoln Barnett calls time and space "forms of intuition"; and he states that they "can no more be divorced from consciousness than can our concept of color, shape and size." Another of today's clear-thinking, clear-seeing mental leaders calls matter "a wave of improbability."

As scholar, philosopher and scientist study the universe in the light of today's broadening knowledge and forward-looking, unshackled desire for truth, their findings are leading them to discredit the old material concepts and even to repudiate matter and support mind as the one great Absolute, the one unchanging and provable force in a cosmos where appearance has for so long veiled fact. The path of the spiritual-minded and the path of those who search for the origin, source, cause and explanation of our universe in the physical realm seem to be converging. The thinker of today has begun to consider materialism as the mist which the second chapter of Genesis declares went up from the face of the earth; and whoever perceives this as fact is able to look through the mist of matter even when it appears dense and stifling.

That mass can be converted into energy was one of the basic propositions used by Dr. Einstein in working out his theory of relativity. Surely energy is nothing a man would expect to taste, touch or hold in his hand! So matter is being deprived of its claim to solidity by physics, by mathematics and even by astronomy. But Jesus "nothingized" matter long ago; and the scholar of today joins the religionist of yesterday in recognizing that the theories of Christ Jesus are as sound and scientific as they are spiritual.

Today's attitude toward matter, and so toward materialism, is summarized in this widely quoted statement by Dr. Edmund W. Sinnott, dean of the Sheffield Scientific School of Yale University: "The good old days of billiard-ball atoms . . . and the indestructibility of matter are now gone. . . . Matter in its old sense has indeed ceased to be."

In a world of relativity a number of man's concepts of life have had to be altered to fit the fact that there is no longer any claim to the Absolute in the physical realm or in theories about it.

The universe simply cannot be understood in terms of the material senses. Many of us are constantly proving this for ourselves and on the minuscule scale of our own perceptions. We know the mirage for what it is. We have been educated to understand that much of what seems to be going on is only a misperception of actuality—an optical illusion. It remains for us to become aware of the riches, the spiritual blessings all around us, imperceptible to eyes still intent on the worldly riches mankind has craved and fought for during all the dark ages when the mist of matter appeared to cover everything.

Here is a simple little tale which exemplifies the difference between spiritual vision and material seeing.

Not long ago I visited a friend at the country place

from which, after several years of bitter struggle, she had begun to wrest a comfortable living for herself, her crippled husband and their two little girls.

Amelia's jellies and preserves are doing well, but she has not quite forgotten the days when she lived in constant fear that the orchards would not bear.

One afternoon Mardie, aged three, and her eight-year-old sister, Caroline, took me down to see the cherry orchard, and at sight of the clouds of beauty on the trees the little one ran toward them shouting, "Mardie want! Mardie pick lots and take to Papa! Mardie wants lots a f'owers in her house!"

Caroline raced after her sister, protesting, "No, darling! Mama can't afford to waste a single cherry. Papa will ride down to see them in his chair. He says he loves to see the blossoms on the trees. Yesterday he told Mama he could see the fruit in the blossom and the cherries in the jars and the mortgage lifted right off the house. But there won't be enough for all that if you pick lotsa blossoms."

Presumably Caroline did not know all she was implying, and in any case Mardie wasn't tall enough to reach more than three or four branches in the whole orchard. The little one contented herself with scooping up petals from the grass, and I contented myself with the fact that a frail man in a wheel chair could see the "fruit in the blossom" and that he had an awareness of mind's provision. For this means that perhaps someday he will recognize that an idea from the source of ideas showed Amelia how to gather blessings from a seemingly run-down farm, and then it should not be difficult for him to recognize that mind can also rehabilitate a body which appears to be run down.

The abundance of fruit which their land is now supplying for Amelia's growing enterprise was always a potential of the fertile ground and the neglected trees. All that was needed was a constructive idea. When it came to Amelia, she used it; she was able to REAL-ize the potentialities of the old farm, and it yielded an abundant supply for her family's needs.

Our world—yours and mine—is filled with "fruit in the blossom" which does not avail us in the least unless and until we become aware of it. Our relation to creative intelligence and its inspirations is actual, and we need only make it factual in order to reap its benefits, whether that be a glorious harvest of cherries and peaches and pears and apples or a crooked body made straight and lifted out of a wheel chair. For as it is written in Philippians 4:13:

> I can do all things through Christ which strengtheneth me.

The keys of the kingdom are in the hands of the man or the woman who is aware that Heaven is not a place but a state of mind.

18

THOUGHTS RULE THE WORLD

We look to Thee; Thy truth is still the Light
Which guides the nations, groping on their way,
Stumbling and falling in disastrous night,
Yet ever hoping for the perfect day.

—THEODORE PARKER,
"The Way, the Truth, and the Life"

"GREAT men are they who see that spiritual is stronger than material force; that thoughts rule the world." Ralph Waldo Emerson made this statement in an address, "Progress of Culture," which he delivered before the Phi Beta Kappa society shortly following the Civil War.

That unhappy period was one of conflict between two ways of thought. Today we are trying to solve a far more exaggerated divergence of thought—the gap between the idealism which includes respect for the individual and the "practical materialism" which is ready to sacrifice humanity to gain its purpose.

The claim that right is might and that it is earth's dominant power takes issue not only with the truth of being but with the evidence of history. Human ambition has always run amok when it was setting out to conquer the world. But it has never been able to carry out its purpose, so it is not unnatural to believe that it never will succeed.

A menace does not of itself inflict so much harm as the terror of it imposes. Threats of fear cause panic, panic leads to stampede, and in a stampede men trample one another to death as they run blindly from a holocaust which they might have escaped if they had not blocked their own exits to safety.

A primitive mountaineer who rescued the only survivors of a flash flood which swept through his valley was asked how it felt to be a hero.

"Don't know anything 'bout this hero idee," he replied. "How I feel is like there's more to me than ever I'd suspected an' as if God was a sight closer than ever I'd expected."

God is much nearer to us than some of us recognize. We would think better of ourselves and our equipment to meet life on whatever terms it is presented if we thought more of God and our relation to Him. The man who acknowledges himself as made in the image and likeness of God (Genesis 1:27) is bound to view himself and his endowment with a confidence quite impossible to the man who believes that he was made of the dust of the ground (Genesis 2:7).

The "dust man" is conditioned by his sense of origin and composition. He identifies himself with perishable matter in its lowest state. So it is logical for him to expect destruction and probably disintegration when wind or flood or fire start bearing down on him.

The man who fancies himself descended from Adam and Adam made from a handful of dust scooped up from the ground is no better off than the savage who believes the Indian legend of how Great Spirit created the races of mankind. The story goes like this:

"First Great Spirit made man out of mud and bake him in oven. Bake him too little, so he not done, he dough. He white man. Great Spirit sigh, take more mud, make another clay man and bake. Bake too much. So he get black man, soft like charcoal. Great Spirit shake head and try again. This time he very careful: He take just right size lump clay; he mold slow and smooth; he watch oven so he bake just enough. Now he get fine, strong man, so he satisfied. He get red man!"

All men have great need of knowing themselves to be the sons of God—"And if children, then heirs; heirs of God, and joint-heirs with Christ"—for without this knowledge and the confidence it gives the challenge of our day is almost too great to meet.

Actually it is our thought about things and not the things themselves—nor any quality inherent in them—which makes them delightful or repulsive, comforting or irritating to us as individuals. We can prove the truth of this to ourselves by the simplest of illustrations: Mary dislikes strawberries but thinks raspberries are delicious; John likes chocolate ice cream, and his twin brother, Jerry, demands coffee flavor. In the minor as well as in the major conditions of our day each one approaches everything from the angle of his own reactions to it, his own thought about it.

A physicist of great eminence once declared that the apparent imperfection of our world was "no longer to be interpreted as evil, but only as imperfect apprehension."

It is perfect apprehension for which we must strive. We want to understand, to comprehend life, not to accept biased impressions and imperfect concepts of what is going on around us. And it is possible for any of us who will to become aware of the real, the true and the good instead of letting distortions of them be foisted on him as actual.

When young Solomon inherited the throne of his father, David, he recognized that he had received a great heritage and must meet a great challenge. He did not start out by swaggering and posturing before his world, as many a young prince is tempted to do when he finds himself king, nor did he go to the other extreme and become panicky over his burdens and obligations. Solomon approached his task with a sense that he was "but a little child" who did not know how to go out or to come in! So he turned to God with an earnest prayer for an understanding heart. His humble prayer for God's help, his deep desire for wisdom, so that he might be fit to govern a great people, brought him far more than he had asked.

The challenge Solomon had to meet was expressed in very different terms from the temptations David had to face. And yet, in essence, the problem was the same for father and son. It is always the same for those who are suddenly elevated to positions of importance and who find themselves faced with a sense of being unready, unequipped, inexperienced and, therefore, afraid.

The challenge that comes to every man, even as it came to the two great kings of Israel, is objectified in many ways. It may appear as brute force, the equivalent of the lion or the bear which attacked David's flocks when he was a simple shepherd boy. It may come as a twentieth-century Goliath of Gath boasting of his might and scornfully demanding that a champion step forth and try to stand against him. It may materialize itself as envy and jealousy preparing to do away with a rival as King Saul tried to do when the young minstrel whose songs could lull him to sleep turned into a hero and a popular idol.

Though he lived in an age of idolatry, corruption and oppression the prophet Micah was able to declare:

> Rejoice not against me, O mine enemy: when I fall, I shall arise; when I sit in darkness, the Lord shall be a light unto me.

This is the word of a man of vision who saw in his day, as we are trying to perceive in ours, that confidence in good is not to be defeated by circumstance, however terrifying. He was aware that there is no challenge which cannot be met by the man who trusts in the power and presence of mind and who relies on the love of God to support him, light his way and reveal the truth which can lead him out of his difficulties.

Nobody invented truth. The spiritual facts about the universe were true even before the seventy-year-old Abram recognized that there is one God and no other and that men have no need to fear, placate or cajole any lesser power. Because he knew this, he was not afraid to leave the familiar country where he was prosperously established and to journey into unknown lands.

The man who understands that the Creator must be good, constructive, beneficent, loving and wise, that there can be only one Creator, or source, and that this power is God cannot be afraid. He knows that God will not harm His creation and that since God never made any power opposed to Himself and His rule, there is nothing other than a diseased imagination which can harm God's image and likeness. Aware of this, entrenched in it, man is ready to meet the challenge of our controversial world.

The insecurity of that world comes from our stubborn insistence that there is a power opposed to God. It does not seem plausible that any who have studied the Bible, or who have reasoned thoughtfully, or who have informed themselves about the conclusions of great thinkers can believe that there is another and deliberately malicious power operating in defiance of the All-Powerful and Almighty, creative mind. It is at least absurd to imagine that God made man in His own likeness and then washed His hands of His creation.

Omnipotence is responsible for its world; omniscience is always aware of its creation. And we, you and I, are responsible for our reaction to these primal facts. We can make everything of them, and so of ourselves, or we can make nothing of them and thus belittle our abilities and powers by belittling their source.

Thoughts rule the world. We have dominion over our own thinking, and the most violent atheist will never deny this. We can choose whom we will serve, what we will think, and, so, what we will be.

But how can we live at peace with the external world if we wage constant warfare against the world within our own consciousness? We need to build up within our own organized, controlled thinking a concept of self, of man as the witness to God and the agent for God. Until we do we are not keeping in touch with the source of our being, God.

When and as we come to REAL-ize that spiritual is stronger than material force, we will begin to deal with one aspect of unbelief: the aspect which derives from fear and its blind panic. Most of us have known fear, but we need not continue the acquaintance unless we choose. The ideal state is never to begin it. This was illustrated simply but conclusively by a little episode which took place a summer ago at a lakeside swimming club.

One afternoon a woman and three children walked across the lawn serenely and with an air of belonging, while a group on the club veranda speculated on who the newcomers were. The two little boys, who looked about five and seven, raced down to the shore, ran out to the end of the dock and dived off with every sign of assurance. Then they swam out toward the float with evident enjoyment and excellent form.

The smallest child, a tiny girl of perhaps three, toddled across the beach on wide-spread, uncertain legs. She did not stop at the rim of the water but went paddling out into it. The onlookers gasped with disapproval and a bit of dismay, but the woman who accompanied the children stood quietly and serenely at the water's edge. She watched the baby, but she did not shout to her to be careful, go splashing after her, or make any attempt to curb the child's activity.

One of the club's leading dowagers protested indignantly that the callous creature's attitude was too outrageous to ignore. Then she marched down from the veranda, crossed the lawn toward the beach, and shouted to the woman, whom she evidently took for a negligent nana.

"Go after that child at once!" shouted the dowager. "She's much too small to be allowed in the water all by herself."

The woman at the water's margin called to one of the little boys, "Look after sister, Jock!" Then she turned and spoke gently to the approaching belligerent. "My little daughter is not afraid, and I am not going to introduce her to fear."

Most of us have been introduced to fear; but we need not cultivate the acquaintance of that undesirable unless we choose.

"A man's enemies are . . . of his own house," and a man's house is his consciousness, his thinking. Thoughts rule the world, and our thought about the world rules the part we play in it and gives us fear and torment or joy and dominion. No matter how much we blame fate or circumstance or any other scapegoat it is thought, our own thinking, which determines our life.

19

THE CONCLUSION OF THE WHOLE MATTER

Let us hear the conclusion of the whole matter: Fear God, and keep his commandments: for this is the whole duty of man.

—ECCLESIASTES 12:13

THE grave uncertainties of our times have driven thoughtful men and women to an earnest search for a way of resolving the confusions of the society in which they are living. It is not enough for an individual to solve his individual problems. We live too close to our neighbors for that to suffice. Modern communications have shortened the distances on the map of the world. The once "far-flung Cathay" is now an adjoining country and can lay its problems on your doorstep and mine.

Men of good will are assuming responsibility for their world; men of vision are aware that they must stand or fall together and that survival depends on the measure of their will to do good for all the world.

In the sixth chapter of Ephesians, Paul advised his disciples to put on the whole armor of God that they might be able to withstand the wiles of the Devil.

That armor, as Paul described it, consists of the breastplate of righteousness (right wisdom), the loincloth of truth (ability to discern the difference between simple honesty and subtle trickery), the shoes of the gospel of peace (that gentle leadership which never tramples on the rights of others), the shield of faith (confidence in good), the helmet of salvation (that sense of protection which comes of understanding God's power and might), and the sword of the spirit (which is the word of God).

It is vital for you and me to know that we possess the full armor of God, for we can get its full benefits as soon as we recognize that it is mental equipment.

There is a way to cope with the challenge of our times. There is a way to claim victory when defeat seems imminent. We have found the way when we "lift up our heart with our hands unto God in the heavens." (Lamentations 3:41.) We pursue that way when we add technique to wisdom and hold fast to the inspiration which started us on the way of salvation. This is not the salvation of an afterlife nor what some call the reward of the righteous but a livable plan for salvation here and now.

"It is part of the cure to wish to be cured," according to Seneca. And when men seek deliverance from their own fears what they most need is a faith in basic, creative, constructive good; for that faith can be built to assurance, to a confidence which is so certain of protection that it carries within itself peace and security.

Fear is mental darkness. Salvation is the dawn of light.

You and I need a willingness to "Let this mind be in you, which was also in Christ Jesus." (Philippians 2:5.) When and as we identify ourselves with this mind and with the goodness which is inherent in it, that wisdom which is of God will flow through us, operate in us and inspire us. And so we will find ourselves possessing the poise and wisdom which come of knowing our dominion over negative, destructive thoughts, whatever form they may assume.

We cannot form an alliance with God until we know deep in our hearts that God *is*. We cannot progress and harvest the fruits of our knowing unless we maintain a consciousness of the high estate which belongs to man as the son and heir of the Ruler of the universe.

As our spiritual awareness grows we cannot fail to REAL-ize for ourselves that knowledge is power and that "as he thinketh in his heart, so is he."

Never forget that man is—you and I are—made in the image of creative mind. We represent God and His power here on earth. We witness to spirit. We were created to express truth. By our thought and consequent action we can present proofs of a supreme wisdom and basic cause to men who have not as yet taken cognizance of any but material power and might. So we have an obligation and a responsibility to God and to mankind.

In the very nature of His being, God is unchanging and

eternal. When he finished His work He called it good. The creation of changeless infinity must remain in the status in which the Creator made and established it; it must forever continue as representative of the work God finished and approved when He looked at it and called it good.

So how can the man of God's creating ever turn into something a supreme wisdom did not make and could not have approved? Why should any intelligent being consent to believe the "big lie" which evil, as man or suggestion, is always muttering? How can anyone accept the fable which in one breath declares that man is a miserable thing made of dust and in the next breath insinuates that if the "dust man" will acquaint himself with the fruits of good and evil, he will become as wise as his Maker?

You and I as individuals manifest in our daily contact with our world those qualities, attitudes, reactions and results which we are accepting as our natural way of expressing what we call "me." *So you and I are what we permit ourselves to be.* Then if you accept yourself as a wretched creature formed of "the dust of the ground" and evidencing the dusty qualities of your origin and composition you are prone to all the calamities likely to befall any lump of clay! But if you visualize yourself as the spiritual likeness of mind and conduct yourself accordingly, you will find it natural to express intelligence in action.

The concept of man as inevitably miserable and compulsively sensual cannot force its way into the consciousness of anyone who resolutely bars it out. A suggestion has to be accepted and developed in thought before it can manifest itself as a condition of experience. If nobody sponsors the pretenses of superstition and misperception, they will never be broadcast. If there is no voice to formulate them, there is nothing to sustain them. A thought without a thinker is inconceivable!

A rumor ignored must die. The hint of fear or insecurity cannot grow into panic without someone to pay attention to it and nurture it.

You and I must grasp these generalities and learn to translate them from things that may be true of "him" or "her" to facts that apply to you and me.

Human experience is shaped by the ideas entertained in human consciousness. So what you and I do not accept as our thought cannot unfold in or as our experience.

Happiness, success and security are built on a foundation of joyous, constructive, tolerant, generous and confident concepts. It is vital for us to learn to acknowledge, recognize and so REAL-ize the good we desire and to deny and destroy the evil we fear. If you are looking for a better way of life, begin developing a better concept of yourself. Learn to recognize your true individuality and its relation to the creative mind which is the source of your being. Identify yourself with the man of mind's creating and acknowledge that God maintains and sustains all which he has made.

Good is natural. Jesus never set aside law in order to attain good. He invoked law in order to set aside the belief that there was a manifest evil which could operate in defiance of God.

It is not conceivable that the Omniscient built the universe in order to distort or destroy it. Children make mud pies for the fun of wiping them out and starting over again. Men build houses and tear them down to build better ones. But is it possible to think of God as proceeding by any such trial-and-error process?

Back of the desolation and decay and defeat we imagine, invite, believe inevitable and by the very force of our expectation invite into our experience, hidden from our view by the clouded beliefs with which we shroud our days and their undertakings and right in the place where we behold limited good and accept it as our portion, is the beautiful, bountiful reality of life as the God, who is love, created it: "And God saw every thing that he had made, and, behold, it was very good."

Reasoning from the premise that God is infinite, the only Creator, and that to be God the Deity must be perfect and complete and altogether lovely, we have no destructive force with which to reckon. If you acknowledge the allness of good, then what is evil but a bad dream?

When a man not only seeks good but pursues it faithfully and steadfastly, when he fills his very being with the joyous awareness that good *is* and is *natural,* he makes channels through which the healing currents of universal beauty and power can flow into his receptive selfhood. In this way he lifts his expectation and with it his experience out of the dust. This is logical and also inevitable, because thought cannot at once be occupied by terror and serenity, by pain and peace, by life and death.

And whatever is true for man, men or mankind is true for you and me. General truth applies to every man and so to the specific man who is considering it and learning how to apply it to the individual called "myself."

You and I are striving to learn how to invoke our highest sense of good as a bulwark against our own fears and the fabulous claims of evil to possess mastery over us. We invalidate them by denying them support. But we must go beyond negating what we do not wish to aid and encourage; we must open consciousness to receive the constructive, inspired ideas which come from creative intelligence. And as we "think God's thoughts after him" and let that mind be in us which was also in Christ Jesus, fear can never overwhelm us.

Whenever the law of creative mind is invoked and followed certain results come to pass. There is a natural sequence which starts with a confident sense of good in action. From this comes an awareness of protection, of inspiration and of quiet assurance. All this brings serenity and security and at the last courage to endure until the problems which have grown out of material, earth-bound, anti-Christlike thinking are conquered.

Those who seek, find. Moses found his burning bush and its inspiration. He gained the understanding which enabled him to lead a people out of bondage and into the awareness of freedom which belongs to those who claim it.

An enslaved thought is never free. An inspired thought can never remain in bondage.

This book tells of many who have borne witness, through their experience and their reaction to that experience, to the fact that God *is* and that His help is available in the *now* in which you and I are living, available today even as it was in Biblical times. For in every age men are able, though not always eager or even willing, to seek and find the truth that makes them free.

In the days when Syria warred against Israel, Elisha saw a host of chariots and horses in the mountain and was able to reveal to his servant how God defends those who trust in Him. Perhaps you and I, though inspired by faith, may not be able to uplift our thought to such clear vision; we may not be able to achieve a confident awareness like that which made Jesus sure that a prayer to his Father, God, would bring a host of angels to save him from the cross. But our security and protection are in direct ratio to our expectation of them. And even for the doubting Thomas to whom the record of history seems fabulous and at best symbolic there may be a quickening awareness that *what man can conceive, man can achieve:* "for by faith ye stand." (II Corinthians 1:24.)

This book tells you of many who have borne witness to the power and presence of spirit, God, the loving Father to whom our needs are known and by whom they will be supplied when and as we learn to "wait never doubting," and in confidence that God is indeed the Ever-Present, the

All-Wise, the Omnipotent, the Creator who never deserts the work of His hands. These pages will have accomplished their purpose if they have persuaded you to join with me in praying:

> And let the beauty of the Lord our God be upon us: and establish thou the work of our hands upon us; yea, the work of our hands establish thou it. (Psalm 90:17.)